Dreams – Visions – God Said

SCROLL- JOURNAL

SERVANT STACY

Copyright © 2021 by **SERVANT STACY**

All rights reserved. No part of this publication may be reproduced, distributed or transmitted in any form or by any means, including photocopying, recording, or other electronic or mechanical methods, without the prior written permission of the publisher, except in the case of brief quotations embodied in critical reviews and certain other noncommercial uses permitted by copyright law. For permission requests, write to the publisher, addressed "Attention: Permissions Coordinator," at the address below.

SERVANT STACY/Rejoice Essential Publishing

PO BOX 512

Effingham, SC 29541

www.republishing.org

Unless otherwise indicated, scripture is taken from the King James Version.' The Holy Bible, English Standard Version (ESV) is adapted from the Revised Standard Version of the Bible, copyright Division of Christian Education of the National Council of the Churches of Christ in the U.S.A. All rights reserved.

Scripture quotations marked (NIV) are taken from the Holy Bible, New International Version®, NIV®. Copyright © 1973, 1978, 1984, 2011 by Biblica, Inc.™ Used by permission of Zondervan. All rights reserved worldwide. www.zondervan.comThe "NIV" and "New International Version" are trademarks registered in the United States Patent and Trademark Office by Biblica, Inc.™ Scripture taken from the New King James Version®. Copyright © 1982 by Thomas Nelson. Used by permission. All rights reserved.

Dreams – Visions – God Said/ SERVANT STACY

ISBN-13: 978-1-952312-53-3

These are the latter days, "And it shall come to pass in the last days, saith God, I will pour out of my Spirit upon all flesh: and your sons and your daughters shall prophesy, and your young men shall see visions, and your old men shall dream dreams."- Acts 2:17 KJV

Beloved, I am so glad you decided to pick up this book. This dream journal has been designed to assist you in capturing your visions and dreams. Apostle Stacy Stover is inviting you to journal and hold dear to your heart the instructions revealed to you by our Heavenly Father in your dreams. God speaks to us in dreams and various Scriptures confirm how He meets individuals in the dreamscape to reveal His secrets. Amos 3:7 says, "Surely the Lord GOD will do nothing, but he revealeth his secret unto his servants the prophets."

This journal is your starting point; therefore, consider it your launching pad into a deeper relationship with the Father, as God's heart towards you is unveiled. Next, consider what has been revealed to you during your sleep, write it down, and pray, asking God for deeper meaning and interpretation. There are various things revealed to us in our dreams, so capturing this information is important. Keep this book by your bed with a pen. Jot down whatever you can recall, such as people, colors, structures, locations, rooms, etc. They all have meaning, "For God speaketh once, yea twice, yet man perceiveth it not. In a dream, in a vision of the night, when deep sleep falleth upon men, in slumberings upon the bed; then he openeth the ears of men, and sealeth their instruction, that he may withdraw man from his purpose, and hide pride from man. He keepeth back his soul from the pit, and his life from perishing by the sword." -Job 33:14-18 KJV

I pray the Lord begins to reveal not only His purpose for your life, but I hope that you gain a deeper understanding of the Father's will for your life. For it is indeed the Lord's desire to see you saved, delivered, joyful, and whole.

Blessings,

Apostle Chantell L. Poole, MDIV, BCC

This book is more than a journal but a vision and dream of what God spoke unto Apostle Stacy. Allow the light of the Lord (Psalms 27:1) given unto her to transfer as you capture every supernatural occurrence from the Lord, creating in you more resounding praise, worship, and understanding to open you up to receive the destination designed especially for you. Allow the Lord to transform you into fishers of men that take you into deeper parts of knowledge by placing all the magnificent wonder received from the Lord in one place that you can tap into deeper realms of learning as the Lord reveals.

Dr. Zolisha L Ware
President | Fearless Global Book & Tutorials

Introduction

The Dreams, Vision, and God Said Journal/Scroll was inspired by the Holy Spirit for His sheep according to John 10:27. That includes Dreamers Seers and those that hear His Voice.. We are surely in the last days.

Acts 2:17 (NIV) says, "I will pour out my Spirit on all people. Your sons and daughters will prophesy, your young men will see visions, your old men will dream dreams.

This journal was designed to help us keep an account of our Dreams and Visions in one place. God Says is a bonus to write when He whispers in His Sweet Soft Voice (Your Private Time With Him).

Part One

My Dream

Dream

Ecclesiastes 5:3 (ESV)

For a dream comes with much business, and a fool's voice with many words.

Date: _____

What did you dream?

_____
_____
_____
_____
_____
_____
_____
_____
_____
_____
_____
_____
_____
_____
_____
_____
_____
_____

What stood out within the dream?

Dream Interpretation:

Fulfillment Date of Dream: _____

Dream

Joel 2:28 (ESV)

"And it shall come to pass afterward, that I will pour out my Spirit on all flesh; your sons and your daughters shall prophesy, your old men shall dream dreams, and your young men shall see visions.

Date: _____

What did you dream?

_____
_____
_____
_____
_____
_____
_____
_____
_____
_____
_____
_____
_____

What stood out within the dream?

_____

_____

_____

_____

Dream Interpretation:

_____

_____

_____

_____

_____

_____

_____

_____

_____

_____

_____

_____

_____

_____

_____

_____

_____

Fulfillment Date of Dream: _____

Dream

Numbers 12:6 (ESV)

And he said, "Hear my words: If there is a prophet among you, I the Lord make myself known to him in a vision; I speak with him in a dream.

Date: _____

What did you dream?

_____
_____
_____
_____
_____
_____
_____
_____
_____
_____
_____
_____
_____
_____

Dreams – Visions – God Said

What stood out within the dream?

_____
_____
_____
_____

Dream Interpretation:

_____
_____
_____
_____
_____
_____
_____
_____
_____
_____
_____
_____
_____
_____
_____
_____
_____

Fulfillment Date of Dream: _____

Dream

Acts 2:17 (ESV)

"'And in the last days it shall be, God declares, that I will pour out my Spirit on all flesh, and your sons and your daughters shall prophesy, and your young men shall see visions, and your old men shall dream dreams;

Date: _____

What did you dream?

_____
_____
_____
_____
_____
_____
_____
_____
_____
_____
_____
_____
_____
_____

What stood out within the dream?

___

Dream Interpretation:

___

Fulfillment Date of Dream: ___

Dream

Proverbs 29:18 (ESV)

Where there is no prophetic vision the people cast off restraint, but blessed is he who keeps the law.

Date: _____

What did you dream?

_____
_____
_____
_____
_____
_____
_____
_____
_____
_____
_____
_____
_____
_____
_____

What stood out within the dream?

Dream Interpretation:

Fulfillment Date of Dream: _____

Dream

Job 33:15 (ESV)

In a dream, in a vision of the night, when deep sleep falls on men, while they slumber on their beds,

Date: _____

What did you dream?

_____
_____
_____
_____
_____
_____
_____
_____
_____
_____
_____
_____
_____
_____
_____

What stood out within the dream?

Dream Interpretation:

Fulfillment Date of Dream: _____

Dream

Daniel 1:17 (ESV)

As for these four youths, God gave them learning and skill in all literature and wisdom, and Daniel had understanding in all visions and dreams.

Date: _____

What did you dream?

_____
_____
_____
_____
_____
_____
_____
_____
_____
_____
_____
_____
_____
_____
_____

What stood out within the dream?

Dream Interpretation:

Fulfillment Date of Dream: _____

Dream

Acts 16:9 (ESV)

And a vision appeared to Paul in the night: a man of Macedonia was standing there, urging him and saying, "Come over to Macedonia and help us."

Date: _____

What did you dream?

_____
_____
_____
_____
_____
_____
_____
_____
_____
_____
_____
_____
_____
_____
_____
_____

What stood out within the dream?

_____
_____
_____
_____

Dream Interpretation:

_____
_____
_____
_____
_____
_____
_____
_____
_____
_____
_____
_____
_____
_____
_____
_____
_____
_____

Fulfillment Date of Dream: _____

Dream

1 John 4:1 (ESV)

Beloved, do not believe every spirit, but test the spirits to see whether they are from God, for many false prophets have gone out into the world.

Date: _____

What did you dream?

_____
_____
_____
_____
_____
_____
_____
_____
_____
_____
_____
_____
_____
_____
_____
_____

What stood out within the dream?

_____

_____

_____

_____

Dream Interpretation:

_____

_____

_____

_____

_____

_____

_____

_____

_____

_____

_____

_____

_____

_____

_____

_____

Fulfillment Date of Dream: _____

Dream

Matthew 27:19 (ESV)

Besides, while he was sitting on the judgment seat, his wife sent word to him, "Have nothing to do with that righteous man, for I have suffered much because of him today in a dream."

Date: _____

What did you dream?

_____
_____
_____
_____
_____
_____
_____
_____
_____
_____
_____
_____
_____
_____

What stood out within the dream?

_____

_____

_____

_____

Dream Interpretation:

_____

_____

_____

_____

_____

_____

_____

_____

_____

_____

_____

_____

_____

_____

_____

_____

Fulfillment Date of Dream: _____

Dream

Genesis 46:2 (ESV)

And God spoke to Israel in visions of the night and said, "Jacob, Jacob." And he said, "Here am I."

Date: _____

Date: _____

What did you dream?

_____

_____

_____

_____

_____

_____

_____

_____

_____

_____

_____

_____

_____

_____

What stood out within the dream?

_____

_____

_____

_____

Dream Interpretation:

_____

_____

_____

_____

_____

_____

_____

_____

_____

_____

_____

_____

_____

_____

_____

_____

_____

Fulfillment Date of Dream: _____

Dream

Ecclesiastes 5:7 (ESV)

For when dreams increase and words grow many, there is vanity; but God is the one you must fear.

Date: _____

What did you dream?

_____

_____

_____

_____

_____

_____

_____

_____

_____

_____

_____

_____

_____

What stood out within the dream?

_____

_____

_____

_____

Dream Interpretation:

_____

_____

_____

_____

_____

_____

_____

_____

_____

_____

_____

_____

_____

_____

_____

_____

_____

Fulfillment Date of Dream: _____

Dream

Daniel 2:28 (ESV)

But there is a God in heaven who reveals mysteries, and he has made known to King Nebuchadnezzar what will be in the latter days. Your dream and the visions of your head as you lay in bed are these:

Date: _____

What did you dream?

_____
_____
_____
_____
_____
_____
_____
_____
_____
_____
_____
_____
_____
_____

What stood out within the dream?

_____

_____

_____

_____

Dream Interpretation:

_____

_____

_____

_____

_____

_____

_____

_____

_____

_____

_____

_____

_____

_____

_____

_____

_____

_____

Fulfillment Date of Dream: _____

Dream

Daniel 4:5 (ESV)

I saw a dream that made me afraid. As I lay in bed the fancies and the visions of my head alarmed me.

Date: _____

What did you dream?

_____
_____
_____
_____
_____
_____
_____
_____
_____
_____
_____
_____
_____
_____
_____
_____

What stood out within the dream?

_____

_____

_____

_____

Dream Interpretation:

_____

_____

_____

_____

_____

_____

_____

_____

_____

_____

_____

_____

_____

_____

Fulfillment Date of Dream: _____

Dream

Genesis 15:1 (ESV)

After these things the word of the Lord came to Abram in a vision: "Fear not, Abram, I am your shield; your reward shall be very great."

Date: _____

What did you dream?

_____
_____
_____
_____
_____
_____
_____
_____
_____
_____
_____
_____
_____
_____
_____

What stood out within the dream?

___

Dream Interpretation:

___

Fulfillment Date of Dream: _____

Dream

Matthew 2:13 (ESV)

Now when they had departed, behold, an angel of the Lord appeared to Joseph in a dream and said, "Rise, take the child and his mother, and flee to Egypt, and remain there until I tell you, for Herod is about to search for the child, to destroy him."

Date: _____

What did you dream?

_____
_____
_____
_____
_____
_____
_____
_____
_____
_____
_____
_____
_____

What stood out within the dream?

Dream Interpretation:

Fulfillment Date of Dream: _____

Dream

Jeremiah 23:16 (ESV)

Thus says the Lord of hosts: "Do not listen to the words of the prophets who prophesy to you, filling you with vain hopes. They speak visions of their own minds, not from the mouth of the Lord.

Date: _____

What did you dream?

_____
_____
_____
_____
_____
_____
_____
_____
_____
_____
_____
_____
_____

What stood out within the dream?

Dream Interpretation:

Fulfillment Date of Dream: _____

Dream

Amos 3:7 (ESV)

"For the Lord God does nothing without revealing his secret to his servants the prophets.

Date: _____

What did you dream?

_____
_____
_____
_____
_____
_____
_____
_____
_____
_____
_____
_____
_____
_____
_____
_____

What stood out within the dream?

_____

_____

_____

_____

Dream Interpretation:

_____

_____

_____

_____

_____

_____

_____

_____

_____

_____

_____

_____

_____

_____

_____

_____

Fulfillment Date of Dream: _____

Dream

Habakkuk 2:2 (ESV)

And the Lord answered me: "Write the vision; make it plain on tablets, so he may run who reads it.

Date: _____

What did you dream?

_____
_____
_____
_____
_____
_____
_____
_____
_____
_____
_____
_____
_____
_____
_____

What stood out within the dream?

Dream Interpretation:

Fulfillment Date of Dream: _____

Dream

Matthew 1:20 (ESV)

But as he considered these things, behold, an angel of the Lord appeared to him in a dream, saying, "Joseph, son of David, do not fear to take Mary as your wife, for that which is conceived in her is from the Holy Spirit.

Date: _____

What did you dream?

_____
_____
_____
_____
_____
_____
_____
_____
_____
_____
_____
_____
_____
_____
_____

What stood out within the dream?

Dream Interpretation:

Fulfillment Date of Dream: _____

Dream

Acts 18:9 (ESV)

And the Lord said to Paul one night in a vision, "Do not be afraid, but go on speaking and do not be silent,

Date: _____

What did you dream?

_____
_____
_____
_____
_____
_____
_____
_____
_____
_____
_____
_____
_____
_____

What stood out within the dream?

_____

_____

_____

_____

Dream Interpretation:

_____

_____

_____

_____

_____

_____

_____

_____

_____

_____

_____

_____

_____

_____

_____

_____

Fulfillment Date of Dream: _____

Dream

Daniel 7:1-5 (ESV)

In the first year of Belshazzar king of Babylon, Daniel saw a dream and visions of his head as he lay in his bed. Then he wrote down the dream and told the sum of the matter. Daniel declared, "I saw in my vision by night, and behold, the four winds of heaven were stirring up the great sea. And four great beasts came up out of the sea, different from one another. The first was like a lion and had eagles' wings. Then as I looked its wings were plucked off, and it was lifted up from the ground and made to stand on two feet like a man, and the mind of a man was given to it. And behold, another beast, a second one, like a bear. It was raised up on one side. It had three ribs in its mouth between its teeth; and it was told, 'Arise, devour much flesh.

Date: _____

What did you dream?

_____
_____
_____
_____
_____
_____
_____
_____

_____

_____

_____

What stood out within the dream?

_____

_____

_____

_____

Dream Interpretation:

_____

_____

_____

_____

_____

_____

_____

_____

_____

_____

_____

_____

_____

Fulfillment Date of Dream: _____

Dream

1 Kings 3:5 (ESV)

At Gibeon the Lord appeared to Solomon in a dream by night, and God said, "Ask what I shall give you."

Date: _____

What did you dream?

_____
_____
_____
_____
_____
_____
_____
_____
_____
_____
_____
_____
_____
_____
_____

What stood out within the dream?

_____

_____

_____

_____

Dream Interpretation:

_____

_____

_____

_____

_____

_____

_____

_____

_____

_____

_____

_____

_____

_____

_____

_____

Fulfillment Date of Dream: _____

Dream

Psalm 89:19 (ESV)

Of old you spoke in a vision to your godly one, and said: "I have granted help to one who is mighty; I have exalted one chosen from the people.

Date: _____

What did you dream?

_____
_____
_____
_____
_____
_____
_____
_____
_____
_____
_____
_____
_____
_____
_____

What stood out within the dream?

_____
_____
_____
_____

Dream Interpretation:

_____
_____
_____
_____
_____
_____
_____
_____
_____
_____
_____
_____
_____
_____
_____
_____
_____

Fulfillment Date of Dream: _____

Dream

Daniel 2:1-5 (ESV)

In the second year of the reign of Nebuchadnezzar, Nebuchadnezzar had dreams; his spirit was troubled, and his sleep left him. Then the king commanded that the magicians, the enchanters, the sorcerers, and the Chaldeans be summoned to tell the king his dreams. So they came in and stood before the king. And the king said to them, "I had a dream, and my spirit is troubled to know the dream." Then the Chaldeans said to the king in Aramaic, "O king, live forever! Tell your servants the dream, and we will show the interpretation." The king answered and said to the Chaldeans, "The word from me is firm: if you do not make known to me the dream and its interpretation, you shall be torn limb from limb, and your houses shall be laid in ruins

Date: _____

What did you dream?

_____
_____
_____
_____
_____
_____

_____
_____
_____
_____

What stood out within the dream?
_____
_____
_____
_____

Dream Interpretation:
_____
_____
_____
_____
_____
_____
_____
_____
_____
_____
_____
_____

Fulfillment Date of Dream: _____

Dream

Isaiah 29:8 (ESV)

As when a hungry man dreams he is eating and awakes with his hunger not satisfied, or as when a thirsty man dreams he is drinking and awakes faint, with his thirst not quenched, so shall the multitude of all the nations be that fight against Mount Zion.

Date: _____

What did you dream?

_____
_____
_____
_____
_____
_____
_____
_____
_____
_____
_____
_____

What stood out within the dream?

Dream Interpretation:

Fulfillment Date of Dream: _____

Dream

1 Samuel 3:1 (ESV)

Now the young man Samuel was ministering to the Lord under Eli. And the word of the Lord was rare in those days; there was no frequent vision.

Date: _____

What did you dream?

_____
_____
_____
_____
_____
_____
_____
_____
_____
_____
_____
_____
_____
_____
_____

What stood out within the dream?

_____

_____

_____

_____

Dream Interpretation:

_____

_____

_____

_____

_____

_____

_____

_____

_____

_____

_____

_____

_____

_____

_____

Fulfillment Date of Dream: _____

Dream

Habakkuk 2:2-3 (ESV)

And the Lord answered me: "Write the vision; make it plain on tablets, so he may run who reads it. For still the vision awaits its appointed time; it hastens to the end—it will not lie. If it seems slow, wait for it; it will surely come; it will not delay.

Date: _____

What did you dream?

_____
_____
_____
_____
_____
_____
_____
_____
_____
_____
_____
_____

What stood out within the dream?

Dream Interpretation:

Fulfillment Date of Dream: _____

Dream

Genesis 20:3 (ESV)

But God came to Abimelech in a dream by night and said to him, "Behold, you are a dead man because of the woman whom you have taken, for she is a man's wife."

Date: _____

What did you dream?

_____
_____
_____
_____
_____
_____
_____
_____
_____
_____
_____
_____
_____
_____
_____

What stood out within the dream?

_____

_____

_____

_____

Dream Interpretation:

_____

_____

_____

_____

_____

_____

_____

_____

_____

_____

_____

_____

_____

_____

_____

_____

Fulfillment Date of Dream: _____

Dream

Genesis 41:1-5 (ESV)

After two whole years, Pharaoh dreamed that he was standing by the Nile, and behold, there came up out of the Nile seven cows attractive and plump, and they fed in the reed grass. And behold, seven other cows, ugly and thin, came up out of the Nile after them, and stood by the other cows on the bank of the Nile. And the ugly, thin cows ate up the seven attractive, plump cows. And Pharaoh awoke. And he fell asleep and dreamed a second time. And behold, seven ears of grain, plump and good, were growing on one stalk

Date: _____

What did you dream?

_____
_____
_____
_____
_____
_____
_____
_____
_____
_____

What stood out within the dream?

_____

_____

_____

_____

Dream Interpretation:

_____

_____

_____

_____

_____

_____

_____

_____

_____

_____

_____

_____

_____

_____

_____

Fulfillment Date of Dream: _____

Dream

Acts 2:1-5 (ESV)

When the day of Pentecost arrived, they were all together in one place. And suddenly there came from heaven a sound like a mighty rushing wind, and it filled the entire house where they were sitting. And divided tongues as of fire appeared to them and rested on each one of them. And they were all filled with the Holy Spirit and began to speak in other tongues as the Spirit gave them utterance. Now there were dwelling in Jerusalem Jews, devout men from every nation under heaven.

Date: _____

What did you dream?

_____
_____
_____
_____
_____
_____
_____
_____
_____
_____

What stood out within the dream?

Dream Interpretation:

Fulfillment Date of Dream: _____

Dream

Genesis 31:24 (ESV)

But God came to Laban the Aramean in a dream by night and said to him, "Be careful not to say anything to Jacob, either good or bad."

Date: _____

What did you dream?

_____
_____
_____
_____
_____
_____
_____
_____
_____
_____
_____
_____
_____
_____
_____
_____
_____

What stood out within the dream?

Dream Interpretation:

Fulfillment Date of Dream: _____

Dream

Daniel 4:1-5 (ESV)

King Nebuchadnezzar to all peoples, nations, and languages, that dwell in all the earth: Peace be multiplied to you! It has seemed good to me to show the signs and wonders that the Most High God has done for me. How great are his signs, how mighty his wonders! His kingdom is an everlasting kingdom, and his dominion endures from generation to generation. I, Nebuchadnezzar, was at ease in my house and prospering in my palace. I saw a dream that made me afraid. As I lay in bed the fancies and the visions of my head alarmed me.

Date: _____

What did you dream?

_____
_____
_____
_____
_____
_____
_____
_____

_____

_____

_____

What stood out within the dream?

_____

_____

_____

_____

Dream Interpretation:

_____

_____

_____

_____

_____

_____

_____

_____

_____

_____

_____

_____

Fulfillment Date of Dream: _____

Dream

Daniel 7:1 (ESV)

In the first year of Belshazzar king of Babylon, Daniel saw a dream and visions of his head as he lay in his bed. Then he wrote down the dream and told the sum of the matter.

Date: _____

What did you dream?

_____
_____
_____
_____
_____
_____
_____
_____
_____
_____
_____
_____
_____
_____

What stood out within the dream?

_____

_____

_____

_____

Dream Interpretation:

_____

_____

_____

_____

_____

_____

_____

_____

_____

_____

_____

_____

_____

_____

_____

_____

Fulfillment Date of Dream: _____

Dream

Joel 2:1-5 (ESV)

Blow a trumpet in Zion; sound an alarm on my holy mountain! Let all the inhabitants of the land tremble, for the day of the Lord is coming; it is near, a day of darkness and gloom, a day of clouds and thick darkness! Like blackness there is spread upon the mountains a great and powerful people; their like has never been before, nor will be again after them through the years of all generations. Fire devours before them, and behind them a flame burns. The land is like the garden of Eden before them, but behind them a desolate wilderness, and nothing escapes them. Their appearance is like the appearance of horses, and like war horses they run. As with the rumbling of chariots, they leap on the tops of the mountains, like the crackling of a flame of fire devouring the stubble, like a powerful army drawn up for battle.

Date: _____

What did you dream?

_____
_____
_____
_____
_____
_____
_____

_____

_____

_____

_____

What stood out within the dream?

_____

_____

_____

_____

Dream Interpretation:

_____

_____

_____

_____

_____

_____

_____

_____

_____

_____

_____

_____

_____

Fulfillment Date of Dream: _____

Dream

Genesis 37:1-5 (ESV)

Jacob lived in the land of his father's sojournings, in the land of Canaan. These are the generations of Jacob. Joseph, being seventeen years old, was pasturing the flock with his brothers. He was a boy with the sons of Bilhah and Zilpah, his father's wives. And Joseph brought a bad report of them to their father. Now Israel loved Joseph more than any other of his sons, because he was the son of his old age. And he made him a robe of many colors. But when his brothers saw that their father loved him more than all his brothers, they hated him and could not speak peacefully to him. Now Joseph had a dream, and when he told it to his brothers they hated him even more.

Date: _____

What did you dream?

_____
_____
_____
_____
_____
_____
_____

_____
_____
_____
_____

What stood out within the dream?

_____
_____
_____
_____

Dream Interpretation:

_____
_____
_____
_____
_____
_____
_____
_____
_____
_____
_____
_____

Fulfillment Date of Dream: _____

Dream

Hebrews 1:1-2 (ESV)

Long ago, at many times and in many ways, God spoke to our fathers by the prophets, but in these last days he has spoken to us by his Son, whom he appointed the heir of all things, through whom also he created the world.

Date: _____

What did you dream?

_____
_____
_____
_____
_____
_____
_____
_____
_____
_____
_____
_____
_____

_____

_____

What stood out within the dream?

_____

_____

_____

_____

Dream Interpretation:

_____

_____

_____

_____

_____

_____

_____

_____

_____

_____

_____

_____

_____

_____

Fulfillment Date of Dream: _____

Dream

Ezekiel 1:1 (ESV)

In the thirtieth year, in the fourth month, on the fifth day of the month, as I was among the exiles by the Chebar canal, the heavens were opened, and I saw visions of God.

Date: _____

What did you dream?

_____
_____
_____
_____
_____
_____
_____
_____
_____
_____
_____
_____
_____
_____

What stood out within the dream?

Dream Interpretation:

Fulfillment Date of Dream: _____

Dream

Daniel 7:15 (ESV)

"As for me, Daniel, my spirit within me was anxious, and the visions of my head alarmed me.

Date: _____

What did you dream?

_____
_____
_____
_____
_____
_____
_____
_____
_____
_____
_____
_____
_____
_____
_____

What stood out within the dream?

Dream Interpretation:

Fulfillment Date of Dream: _____

Dream

Hebrews 1:1 (ESV)

Long ago, at many times and in many ways, God spoke to our fathers by the prophets,

Date: _____

What did you dream?

_____
_____
_____
_____
_____
_____
_____
_____
_____
_____
_____
_____
_____
_____
_____

What stood out within the dream?

Dream Interpretation:

Fulfillment Date of Dream: _____

Dream

Genesis 40:1-5 (ESV)

Sometime after this, the cupbearer of the king of Egypt and his baker committed an offense against their lord the king of Egypt. And Pharaoh was angry with his two officers, the chief cupbearer and the chief baker, and he put them in custody in the house of the captain of the guard, in the prison where Joseph was confined. The captain of the guard appointed Joseph to be with them, and he attended them. They continued for some time in custody. And one night they both dreamed—the cupbearer and the baker of the king of Egypt, who were confined in the prison—each his own dream, and each dream with its own interpretation.

Date: _____

What did you dream?

_____

_____

_____

_____

_____

_____

_____

_____

Dreams – Visions – God Said

_____

_____

_____

What stood out within the dream?

_____

_____

_____

_____

Dream Interpretation:

_____

_____

_____

_____

_____

_____

_____

_____

_____

_____

_____

_____

Fulfillment Date of Dream: _____

Dream

Judges 7:13-15 (ESV)

When Gideon came, behold, a man was telling a dream to his comrade. And he said, "Behold, I dreamed a dream, and behold, a cake of barley bread tumbled into the camp of Midian and came to the tent and struck it so that it fell and turned it upside down, so that the tent lay flat." And his comrade answered, "This is no other than the sword of Gideon the son of Joash, a man of Israel; God has given into his hand Midian and all the camp." As soon as Gideon heard the telling of the dream and its interpretation, he worshiped. And he returned to the camp of Israel and said, "Arise, for the Lord has given the host of Midian into your hand."

Date: _____

What did you dream?

_____
_____
_____
_____
_____
_____
_____
_____
_____

What stood out within the dream?

Dream Interpretation:

Fulfillment Date of Dream: _____

Dream

Matthew 2:12 (ESV)

And being warned in a dream not to return to Herod, they departed to their own country by another way.

Date: _____

What did you dream?

_____
_____
_____
_____
_____
_____
_____
_____
_____
_____
_____
_____
_____
_____
_____
_____

Dreams – Visions – God Said

What stood out within the dream?

_____
_____
_____
_____

Dream Interpretation:

_____
_____
_____
_____
_____
_____
_____
_____
_____
_____
_____
_____
_____
_____
_____
_____
_____
_____

Fulfillment Date of Dream: _____

Dream

Acts 16:9-10 (ESV)

And a vision appeared to Paul in the night: a man of Macedonia was standing there, urging him and saying, "Come over to Macedonia and help us." And when Paul had seen the vision, immediately we sought to go on into Macedonia, concluding that God had called us to preach the gospel to them.

Date: _____

What did you dream?

_____
_____
_____
_____
_____
_____
_____
_____
_____
_____
_____

What stood out within the dream?

Dream Interpretation:

Fulfillment Date of Dream: _____

Dream

Genesis 40:8 (ESV)

They said to him, "We have had dreams, and there is no one to interpret them." And Joseph said to them, "Do not interpretations belong to God? Please tell them to me."

Date: _____

What did you dream?

_____
_____
_____
_____
_____
_____
_____
_____
_____
_____
_____
_____
_____
_____
_____

What stood out within the dream?

_____

_____

_____

_____

Dream Interpretation:

_____

_____

_____

_____

_____

_____

_____

_____

_____

_____

_____

_____

_____

_____

_____

_____

Fulfillment Date of Dream: _____

Dream

Daniel 7:13 (ESV)

"I saw in the night visions, and behold, with the clouds of heaven there came one like a son of man, and he came to the Ancient of Days and was presented before him.

Date: _____

What did you dream?

_____
_____
_____
_____
_____
_____
_____
_____
_____
_____
_____
_____
_____
_____

Dreams – Visions – God Said

What stood out within the dream?

_____
_____
_____
_____

Dream Interpretation:

_____
_____
_____
_____
_____
_____
_____
_____
_____
_____
_____
_____
_____
_____
_____
_____
_____

Fulfillment Date of Dream: _____

Dream

Daniel 7:7 (ESV)

After this I saw in the night visions, and behold, a fourth beast, terrifying and dreadful and exceedingly strong. It had great iron teeth; it devoured and broke in pieces and stamped what was left with its feet. It was different from all the beasts that were before it, and it had ten horns.

Date: _____

What did you dream?

_____
_____
_____
_____
_____
_____
_____
_____
_____
_____
_____
_____

What stood out within the dream?

Dream Interpretation:

Fulfillment Date of Dream: _____

Dream

Deuteronomy 13:1-3 (ESV)

"If a prophet or a dreamer of dreams arises among you and gives you a sign or a wonder, and the sign or wonder that he tells you comes to pass, and if he says, 'Let us go after other gods,' which you have not known, 'and let us serve them,' you shall not listen to the words of that prophet or that dreamer of dreams. For the Lord your God is testing you, to know whether you love the Lord your God with all your heart and with all your soul.

Date: _____

What did you dream?

_____
_____
_____
_____
_____
_____
_____
_____
_____
_____
_____

What stood out within the dream?

Dream Interpretation:

Fulfillment Date of Dream: _____

Dream

Habakkuk 2:3 (ESV)

For still the vision awaits its appointed time; it hastens to the end—it will not lie. If it seems slow, wait for it; it will surely come; it will not delay.

Date: _____

What did you dream?

_____
_____
_____
_____
_____
_____
_____
_____
_____
_____
_____
_____
_____
_____

What stood out within the dream?

_____
_____
_____
_____

Dream Interpretation:

_____
_____
_____
_____
_____
_____
_____
_____
_____
_____
_____
_____
_____
_____
_____
_____

Fulfillment Date of Dream: _____

Dream

Acts 10:17 (ESV)

Now while Peter was inwardly perplexed as to what the vision that he had seen might mean, behold, the men who were sent by Cornelius, having made inquiry for Simon's house, stood at the gate.

Date: _____

What did you dream?

_____
_____
_____
_____
_____
_____
_____
_____
_____
_____
_____
_____
_____
_____

What stood out within the dream?

Dream Interpretation:

Fulfillment Date of Dream: _____

Dream

Jeremiah 14:14 (ESV)

And the Lord said to me: "The prophets are prophesying lies in my name. I did not send them, nor did I command them or speak to them. They are prophesying to you a lying vision, worthless divination, and the deceit of their own minds.

Date: _____

What did you dream?

_____
_____
_____
_____
_____
_____
_____
_____
_____
_____
_____
_____

_____

_____

What stood out within the dream?

_____

_____

_____

_____

Dream Interpretation:

_____

_____

_____

_____

_____

_____

_____

_____

_____

_____

_____

_____

_____

Fulfillment Date of Dream: _____

Dream

Isaiah 1:1 (ESV)

The vision of Isaiah the son of Amoz, which he saw concerning Judah and Jerusalem in the days of Uzziah, Jotham, Ahaz, and Hezekiah, kings of Judah.

Date: _____

What did you dream?

_____
_____
_____
_____
_____
_____
_____
_____
_____
_____
_____
_____
_____
_____

What stood out within the dream?

_____

_____

_____

_____

Dream Interpretation:

_____

_____

_____

_____

_____

_____

_____

_____

_____

_____

_____

_____

_____

_____

_____

Fulfillment Date of Dream: _____

Dream

Daniel 10:14 (ESV)

And came to make you understand what is to happen to your people in the latter days. For the vision is for days yet to come."

Date: _____

What did you dream?

_____
_____
_____
_____
_____
_____
_____
_____
_____
_____
_____
_____
_____
_____
_____

What stood out within the dream?

_____

_____

_____

_____

Dream Interpretation:

_____

_____

_____

_____

_____

_____

_____

_____

_____

_____

_____

_____

_____

_____

_____

_____

_____

Fulfillment Date of Dream: _____

Dream

Nahum 1:1 (ESV)

An oracle concerning Nineveh. The book of the vision of Nahum of Elkosh.

Date: _____

What did you dream?

_____
_____
_____
_____
_____
_____
_____
_____
_____
_____
_____
_____
_____
_____
_____
_____
_____

What stood out within the dream?

_____
_____
_____
_____

Dream Interpretation:

_____
_____
_____
_____
_____
_____
_____
_____
_____
_____
_____
_____
_____
_____
_____
_____

Fulfillment Date of Dream: _____

Dream

Zechariah 10:2 (ESV)

For the household gods utter nonsense, and the diviners see lies; they tell false dreams and give empty consolation. Therefore, the people wander like sheep; they are afflicted for lack of a shepherd.

Date: _____

What did you dream?

_____
_____
_____
_____
_____
_____
_____
_____
_____
_____
_____
_____

_____

_____

What stood out within the dream?

_____

_____

_____

_____

Dream Interpretation:

_____

_____

_____

_____

_____

_____

_____

_____

_____

_____

_____

_____

_____

_____

Fulfillment Date of Dream: _____

Dream

Acts 2:15 (ESV)

For these people are not drunk, as you suppose, since it is only the third hour of the day.

Date: _____

What did you dream?

_____
_____
_____
_____
_____
_____
_____
_____
_____
_____
_____
_____
_____
_____
_____
_____
_____
_____

Dreams – Visions – God Said

What stood out within the dream?

___

Dream Interpretation:

___

Fulfillment Date of Dream: ___

Dream

Obadiah 1:1 (ESV)

The vision of Obadiah. Thus says the Lord God concerning Edom: We have heard a report from the Lord, and a messenger has been sent among the nations: "Rise up! Let us rise against her for battle!"

Date: _____

What did you dream?

_____
_____
_____
_____
_____
_____
_____
_____
_____
_____
_____
_____
_____
_____

What stood out within the dream?

_____

_____

_____

_____

Dream Interpretation:

_____

_____

_____

_____

_____

_____

_____

_____

_____

_____

_____

_____

_____

_____

_____

_____

Fulfillment Date of Dream: _____

Dream

Acts 9:10 (ESV)

Now there was a disciple at Damascus named Ananias. The Lord said to him in a vision, "Ananias." And he said, "Here I am, Lord."

Date: _____

What did you dream?

_____
_____
_____
_____
_____
_____
_____
_____
_____
_____
_____
_____
_____
_____
_____

What stood out within the dream?

Dream Interpretation:

Fulfillment Date of Dream: _____

Dream

Matthew 2:19 (ESV)

But when Herod died, behold, an angel of the Lord appeared in a dream to Joseph in Egypt,

Date: _____

What did you dream?

_____
_____
_____
_____
_____
_____
_____
_____
_____
_____
_____
_____
_____
_____
_____
_____
_____

What stood out within the dream?

Dream Interpretation:

Fulfillment Date of Dream: _____

Dream

Daniel 2:1 (ESV)

In the second year of the reign of Nebuchadnezzar, Nebuchadnezzar had dreams; his spirit was troubled, and his sleep left him.

Date: _____

What did you dream?

_____
_____
_____
_____
_____
_____
_____
_____
_____
_____
_____
_____
_____
_____

What stood out within the dream?

_____
_____
_____
_____

Dream Interpretation:

_____
_____
_____
_____
_____
_____
_____
_____
_____
_____
_____
_____
_____
_____
_____
_____

Fulfillment Date of Dream: _____

Dream

Hosea 12:10 (ESV)

I spoke to the prophets; it was I who multiplied visions, and through the prophets gave parables.

Date: _____

What did you dream?

_____
_____
_____
_____
_____
_____
_____
_____
_____
_____
_____
_____
_____
_____

What stood out within the dream?

_____

_____

_____

_____

Dream Interpretation:

_____

_____

_____

_____

_____

_____

_____

_____

_____

_____

_____

_____

_____

_____

_____

_____

Fulfillment Date of Dream: _____

Dream

Revelation 9:17 (ESV)

And this is how I saw the horses in my vision and those who rode them: they wore breastplates the color of fire and of sapphire and of sulfur, and the heads of the horses were like lions' heads, and fire and smoke and sulfur came out of their mouths.

Date: _____

What did you dream?

_____
_____
_____
_____
_____
_____
_____
_____
_____
_____

What stood out within the dream?

Dream Interpretation:

Fulfillment Date of Dream: _____

Dream

Psalm 23:1-5 (ESV)

A Psalm of David. The Lord is my shepherd; I shall not want. He makes me lie down in green pastures. He leads me beside still waters. He restores my soul. He leads me in paths of righteousness for his name's sake. Even though I walk through the valley of the shadow of death, I will fear no evil, for you are with me; your rod and your staff, they comfort me. You prepare a table before me in the presence of my enemies; you anoint my head with oil; my cup overflows.

Date: _____

What did you dream?

_____
_____
_____
_____
_____
_____
_____
_____
_____
_____

What stood out within the dream?

Dream Interpretation:

Fulfillment Date of Dream: _____

Dream

Daniel 8:18 (ESV)

And when he had spoken to me, I fell into a deep sleep with my face to the ground. But he touched me and made me stand up.

Date: _____

What did you dream?

_____
_____
_____
_____
_____
_____
_____
_____
_____
_____
_____
_____
_____
_____
_____
_____

What stood out within the dream?

_____

_____

_____

_____

Dream Interpretation:

_____

_____

_____

_____

_____

_____

_____

_____

_____

_____

_____

_____

_____

_____

_____

_____

Fulfillment Date of Dream: _____

Dream

Revelation 1:1 (ESV)

The revelation of Jesus Christ, which God gave him to show to his servants the things that must soon take place. He made it known by sending his angel to his servant John,

Date: _____

What did you dream?

_____
_____
_____
_____
_____
_____
_____
_____
_____
_____
_____
_____
_____

What stood out within the dream?

Dream Interpretation:

Fulfillment Date of Dream: _____

Dream

Luke 24:23 (ESV)

And when they did not find his body, they came back saying that they had even seen a vision of angels, who said that he was alive.

Date: _____

What did you dream?

_____
_____
_____
_____
_____
_____
_____
_____
_____
_____
_____
_____
_____
_____
_____
_____

What stood out within the dream?

_____
_____
_____
_____

Dream Interpretation:

_____
_____
_____
_____
_____
_____
_____
_____
_____
_____
_____
_____
_____
_____
_____
_____

Fulfillment Date of Dream: _____

Dream

2 Timothy 3:16-17 (ESV)

All Scripture is breathed out by God and profitable for teaching, for reproof, for correction, and for training in righteousness, that the man of God may be competent, equipped for every good work.

Date: _____

What did you dream?

_____
_____
_____
_____
_____
_____
_____
_____
_____
_____
_____
_____
_____

What stood out within the dream?

Dream Interpretation:

Fulfillment Date of Dream: _____

Dream

Acts 9:10-12 (ESV)

Now there was a disciple at Damascus named Ananias. The Lord said to him in a vision, "Ananias." And he said, "Here I am, Lord." And the Lord said to him, "Rise and go to the street called Straight, and at the house of Judas look for a man of Tarsus named Saul, for behold, he is praying, and he has seen in a vision a man named Ananias come in and lay his hands on him so that he might regain his sight."

Date: _____

What did you dream?

_____
_____
_____
_____
_____
_____
_____
_____
_____
_____

What stood out within the dream?

Dream Interpretation:

Fulfillment Date of Dream: _____

Dream

Joel 2:28-31 (ESV)

"And it shall come to pass afterward, that I will pour out my Spirit on all flesh; your sons and your daughters shall prophesy, your old men shall dream dreams, and your young men shall see visions. Even on the male and female servants in those days I will pour out my Spirit. "And I will show wonders in the heavens and on the earth, blood and fire and columns of smoke. The sun shall be turned to darkness, and the moon to blood, before the great and awesome day of the Lord comes.

Date: _____

What did you dream?

_____
_____
_____
_____
_____
_____
_____
_____
_____
_____

What stood out within the dream?

Dream Interpretation:

Fulfillment Date of Dream: _____

Dream

Acts 10:3 (ESV)

About the ninth hour of the day he saw clearly in a vision an angel of God come in and say to him, "Cornelius."

Date: _____

What did you dream?

_____
_____
_____
_____
_____
_____
_____
_____
_____
_____
_____
_____
_____
_____
_____
_____
_____

What stood out within the dream?

Dream Interpretation:

Fulfillment Date of Dream: _____

Dream

Matthew 2:1-5 (ESV)

Now after Jesus was born in Bethlehem of Judea in the days of Herod the king, behold, wise men from the east came to Jerusalem, saying, "Where is he who has been born king of the Jews? For we saw his star when it rose and have come to worship him." When Herod the king heard this, he was troubled, and all Jerusalem with him; and assembling all the chief priests and scribes of the people, he inquired of them where the Christ was to be born. They told him, "In Bethlehem of Judea, for so it is written by the prophet:

Date: _____

What did you dream?

_____
_____
_____
_____
_____
_____
_____
_____
_____
_____

Dreams – Visions – God Said

What stood out within the dream?

Dream Interpretation:

Fulfillment Date of Dream: _____

Dream

James 1:5 (ESV)

If any of you lacks wisdom, let him ask God, who gives generously to all without reproach, and it will be given him.

Date: _____

What did you dream?

_____
_____
_____
_____
_____
_____
_____
_____
_____
_____
_____
_____
_____
_____
_____
_____

What stood out within the dream?

_____
_____
_____
_____

Dream Interpretation:

_____
_____
_____
_____
_____
_____
_____
_____
_____
_____
_____
_____
_____
_____
_____
_____
_____
_____

Fulfillment Date of Dream: _____

Dream

1 Samuel 28:6 (ESV)

And when Saul inquired of the Lord, the Lord did not answer him, either by dreams, or by Urim, or by prophets.

Date: _____

What did you dream?

_____

_____

_____

_____

_____

_____

_____

_____

_____

_____

_____

_____

_____

_____

_____

_____

Dreams – Visions – God Said

What stood out within the dream?

_____

_____

_____

_____

Dream Interpretation:

_____

_____

_____

_____

_____

_____

_____

_____

_____

_____

_____

_____

_____

_____

_____

Fulfillment Date of Dream: _____

Dream

Zechariah 4:2 (ESV)

And he said to me, "What do you see?" I said, "I see, and behold, a lampstand all of gold, with a bowl on the top of it, and seven lamps on it, with seven lips on each of the lamps that are on the top of it.

Date: _____

What did you dream?

_____
_____
_____
_____
_____
_____
_____
_____
_____
_____
_____
_____
_____
_____

What stood out within the dream?

_____
_____
_____
_____

Dream Interpretation:

_____
_____
_____
_____
_____
_____
_____
_____
_____
_____
_____
_____
_____
_____
_____
_____
_____

Fulfillment Date of Dream: _____

Dream

Job 4:13 (ESV)

Amid thoughts from visions of the night, when deep sleep falls on men,

Date: _____

What did you dream?

_____
_____
_____
_____
_____
_____
_____
_____
_____
_____
_____
_____
_____
_____
_____
_____
_____
_____

What stood out within the dream?

_____

_____

_____

_____

Dream Interpretation:

_____

_____

_____

_____

_____

_____

_____

_____

_____

_____

_____

_____

_____

_____

_____

_____

Fulfillment Date of Dream: _____

Dream

Zechariah 6:1 (ESV)

Again I lifted my eyes and saw, and behold, four chariots came out from between two mountains. And the mountains were mountains of bronze.

Date: _____

What did you dream?

_____
_____
_____
_____
_____
_____
_____
_____
_____
_____
_____
_____
_____
_____
_____
_____

What stood out within the dream?

_____
_____
_____
_____

Dream Interpretation:

_____
_____
_____
_____
_____
_____
_____
_____
_____
_____
_____
_____
_____
_____
_____
_____
_____
_____

Fulfillment Date of Dream: _____

Dream

Ezekiel 7:26 (ESV)

Disaster comes upon disaster; rumor follows rumor. They seek a vision from the prophet, while the law perishes from the priest and counsel from the elders.

Date: _____

What did you dream?

_____
_____
_____
_____
_____
_____
_____
_____
_____
_____
_____
_____
_____
_____

What stood out within the dream?

Dream Interpretation:

Fulfillment Date of Dream: _____

Dream

Daniel 8:15 (ESV)

When I, Daniel, had seen the vision, I sought to understand it. And behold, there stood before me one having the appearance of a man.

Date: _____

What did you dream?

_____
_____
_____
_____
_____
_____
_____
_____
_____
_____
_____
_____
_____
_____
_____

What stood out within the dream?

Dream Interpretation:

Fulfillment Date of Dream: _____

Dream

Genesis 28:12 (ESV)

And he dreamed, and behold, there was a ladder set up on the earth, and the top of it reached to heaven. And behold, the angels of God were ascending and descending on it!

Date: _____

What did you dream?

_____
_____
_____
_____
_____
_____
_____
_____
_____
_____
_____
_____
_____

What stood out within the dream?

_____
_____
_____
_____

Dream Interpretation:

_____
_____
_____
_____
_____
_____
_____
_____
_____
_____
_____
_____
_____
_____
_____

Fulfillment Date of Dream: _____

Dream

Daniel 10:7 (ESV)

And I, Daniel, alone saw the vision, for the men who were with me did not see the vision, but a great trembling fell upon them, and they fled to hide themselves.

Date: _____

What did you dream?

_____
_____
_____
_____
_____
_____
_____
_____
_____
_____
_____
_____
_____
_____
_____
_____
_____

What stood out within the dream?

Dream Interpretation:

Fulfillment Date of Dream: _____

Dream

Job 20:8 (ESV)

He will fly away like a dream and not be found; he will be chased away like a vision of the night.

Date: _____

What did you dream?

_____
_____
_____
_____
_____
_____
_____
_____
_____
_____
_____
_____
_____
_____
_____

What stood out within the dream?

_____

_____

_____

_____

Dream Interpretation:

_____

_____

_____

_____

_____

_____

_____

_____

_____

_____

_____

_____

_____

_____

_____

_____

_____

Fulfillment Date of Dream: _____

Dream

Jeremiah 23:28 (ESV)

Let the prophet who has a dream tell the dream, but let him who has my word speak my word faithfully. What has straw in common with wheat? declares the Lord.

Date: _____

What did you dream?

_____
_____
_____
_____
_____
_____
_____
_____
_____
_____
_____
_____
_____
_____
_____

What stood out within the dream?

Dream Interpretation:

Fulfillment Date of Dream: _____

Dream

Ezekiel 12:22 (ESV)

"Son of man, what is this proverb that you have about the land of Israel, saying, 'The days grow long, and every vision comes to nothing'?

Date: _____

What did you dream?

_____
_____
_____
_____
_____
_____
_____
_____
_____
_____
_____
_____
_____
_____
_____

What stood out within the dream?

_____

_____

_____

_____

Dream Interpretation:

_____

_____

_____

_____

_____

_____

_____

_____

_____

_____

_____

_____

_____

_____

_____

_____

Fulfillment Date of Dream: _____

Dream

Acts 9:10-11 (ESV)

Now there was a disciple at Damascus named Ananias. The Lord said to him in a vision, "Ananias." And he said, "Here I am, Lord." And the Lord said to him, "Rise and go to the street called Straight, and at the house of Judas look for a man of Tarsus named Saul, for behold, he is praying,

Date: _____

What did you dream?

_____
_____
_____
_____
_____
_____
_____
_____
_____
_____
_____
_____

What stood out within the dream?

Dream Interpretation:

Fulfillment Date of Dream: _____

Dream

Genesis 41:1-5 (ESV)

After two whole years, Pharaoh dreamed that he was standing by the Nile, and behold, there came up out of the Nile seven cows attractive and plump, and they fed in the reed grass. And behold, seven other cows, ugly and thin, came up out of the Nile after them, and stood by the other cows on the bank of the Nile. And the ugly, thin cows ate up the seven attractive, plump cows.

And Pharaoh awoke. And he fell asleep and dreamed a second time. And behold, seven ears of grain, plump and good, were growing on one stalk.

Date: _____

What did you dream?

_____
_____
_____
_____
_____
_____
_____
_____
_____

_____
_____
_____
_____

What stood out within the dream?

_____
_____
_____
_____

Dream Interpretation:

_____
_____
_____
_____
_____
_____
_____
_____
_____
_____
_____
_____
_____

Fulfillment Date of Dream: _____

Dream

Job 7:14 (ESV)

Then you scare me with dreams and terrify me with visions,

Date: _____

What did you dream?

_____
_____
_____
_____
_____
_____
_____
_____
_____
_____
_____
_____
_____
_____
_____
_____
_____

What stood out within the dream?

_____

_____

_____

_____

Dream Interpretation:

_____

_____

_____

_____

_____

_____

_____

_____

_____

_____

_____

_____

_____

_____

_____

_____

_____

_____

Fulfillment Date of Dream: _____

Dream

2 Chronicles 9:29 (ESV)

Now the rest of the acts of Solomon, from first to last, are they not written in the history of Nathan the prophet, and in the prophecy of Ahijah the Shilonite, and in the visions of Iddo the seer concerning Jeroboam the son of Nebat?

Date: _____

What did you dream?

_____
_____
_____
_____
_____
_____
_____
_____
_____
_____
_____
_____

What stood out within the dream?

Dream Interpretation:

Fulfillment Date of Dream: _____

Dream

Micah 3:6 (ESV)

Therefore it shall be night to you, without vision, and darkness to you, without divination. The sun shall go down on the prophets, and the day shall be black over them;

Date: _____

What did you dream?

_____
_____
_____
_____
_____
_____
_____
_____
_____
_____
_____
_____
_____
_____
_____

What stood out within the dream?

Dream Interpretation:

Fulfillment Date of Dream: _____

Dream

Daniel 8:1 (ESV)

In the third year of the reign of King Belshazzar a vision appeared to me, Daniel, after that which appeared to me at the first.

Date: _____

What did you dream?

_____
_____
_____
_____
_____
_____
_____
_____
_____
_____
_____
_____
_____
_____
_____

What stood out within the dream?

Dream Interpretation:

Fulfillment Date of Dream: _____

Dream

Lamentations 2:9 (ESV)

Her gates have sunk into the ground; he has ruined and broken her bars; her king and princes are among the nations; the law is no more, and her prophets find no vision from the Lord.

Date: _____

What did you dream?

_____
_____
_____
_____
_____
_____
_____
_____
_____
_____
_____
_____

What stood out within the dream?

Dream Interpretation:

Fulfillment Date of Dream: _____

Dream

2 Corinthians 12:1 (ESV)

I must go on boasting. Though there is nothing to be gained by it, I will go on to visions and revelations of the Lord.

Date: _____

What did you dream?

_____
_____
_____
_____
_____
_____
_____
_____
_____
_____
_____
_____
_____
_____
_____
_____
_____

What stood out within the dream?

_____

_____

_____

_____

Dream Interpretation:

_____

_____

_____

_____

_____

_____

_____

_____

_____

_____

_____

_____

_____

_____

_____

_____

Fulfillment Date of Dream: _____

Dream

2 Chronicles 32:32 (ESV)

Now the rest of the acts of Hezekiah and his good deeds, behold, they are written in the vision of Isaiah the prophet the son of Amoz, in the Book of the Kings of Judah and Israel.

Date: _____

What did you dream?

_____
_____
_____
_____
_____
_____
_____
_____
_____
_____
_____
_____
_____
_____

What stood out within the dream?

Dream Interpretation:

Fulfillment Date of Dream: _____

Dream

Daniel 10:1 (ESV)

In the third year of Cyrus king of Persia a word was revealed to Daniel, who was named Belteshazzar. And the word was true, and it was a great conflict. And he understood the word and had understanding of the vision.

Date: _____

What did you dream?

_____
_____
_____
_____
_____
_____
_____
_____
_____
_____
_____
_____
_____
_____
_____

What stood out within the dream?

Dream Interpretation:

Fulfillment Date of Dream: _____

Dream

Job 7:13-14 (ESV)

When I say, 'My bed will comfort me, my couch will ease my complaint,' then you scare me with dreams and terrify me with visions,

Date: _____

What did you dream?

_____
_____
_____
_____
_____
_____
_____
_____
_____
_____
_____
_____
_____
_____

What stood out within the dream?

Dream Interpretation:

Fulfillment Date of Dream: _____

Dream

Daniel 8:26 (ESV)

The vision of the evenings and the mornings that has been told is true, but seal

Date: _____

What did you dream?

_____
_____
_____
_____
_____
_____
_____
_____
_____
_____
_____
_____
_____
_____
_____
_____

What stood out within the dream?

Dream Interpretation:

Fulfillment Date of Dream: _____

Dream

Daniel 11:14 (ESV)

"In those times many shall rise against the king of the south, and the violent among your own people shall lift themselves up in order to fulfill the vision, but they shall fail.

Date: _____

What did you dream?

_____
_____
_____
_____
_____
_____
_____
_____
_____
_____
_____
_____
_____
_____
_____
_____

Dreams – Visions – God Said

What stood out within the dream?

_____

_____

_____

_____

Dream Interpretation:

_____

_____

_____

_____

_____

_____

_____

_____

_____

_____

_____

_____

_____

_____

_____

Fulfillment Date of Dream: _____

Dream

Daniel 8:13 (ESV)

Then I heard a holy one speaking, and another holy one said to the one who spoke, "For how long is the vision concerning the regular burnt offering, the transgression that makes desolate, and the giving over of the sanctuary and host to be trampled underfoot?"

Date: _____

What did you dream?

_____
_____
_____
_____
_____
_____
_____
_____
_____
_____
_____

What stood out within the dream?

Dream Interpretation:

Fulfillment Date of Dream: _____

Dream

Ezekiel 11:24 (ESV)

And the Spirit lifted me up and brought me in the vision by the Spirit of God into Chaldea, to the exiles. Then the vision that I had seen went up from me.

Date: _____

What did you dream?

_____
_____
_____
_____
_____
_____
_____
_____
_____
_____
_____
_____
_____

Dreams – Visions – God Said

What stood out within the dream?

_____
_____
_____
_____

Dream Interpretation:

_____
_____
_____
_____
_____
_____
_____
_____
_____
_____
_____
_____
_____
_____
_____
_____
_____

Fulfillment Date of Dream: _____

Dream

Isaiah 21:2 (ESV)

A stern vision is told to me; the traitor betrays, and the destroyer destroys. Go up, O Elam; lay siege, O Media; all the sighing she has caused I bring to an end.

Date: _____

What did you dream?

_____

_____

_____

_____

_____

_____

_____

_____

_____

_____

_____

_____

_____

_____

_____

_____

What stood out within the dream?

_____

_____

_____

_____

Dream Interpretation:

_____

_____

_____

_____

_____

_____

_____

_____

_____

_____

_____

_____

_____

_____

_____

_____

Fulfillment Date of Dream: _____

Dream

Job 11:2 (ESV)

" "Should a multitude of words go unanswered, and a man full of talk be judged right?

Date: _____

What did you dream?

_____
_____
_____
_____
_____
_____
_____
_____
_____
_____
_____
_____
_____
_____
_____
_____
_____
_____

Dreams – Visions – God Said

What stood out within the dream?

_____

_____

_____

_____

Dream Interpretation:

_____

_____

_____

_____

_____

_____

_____

_____

_____

_____

_____

_____

_____

_____

_____

Fulfillment Date of Dream: _____

Dream

Proverbs 10:19 (ESV)

When words are many, transgression is not lacking, but whoever restrains his lips is prudent.

Date: _____

What did you dream?

_____
_____
_____
_____
_____
_____
_____
_____
_____
_____
_____
_____
_____
_____
_____
_____

What stood out within the dream?

Dream Interpretation:

Fulfillment Date of Dream: _____

Dream

Proverbs 15:2 (ESV)

The tongue of the wise commends knowledge, but the mouths of fools pour out folly.

Date: _____

What did you dream?

_____
_____
_____
_____
_____
_____
_____
_____
_____
_____

What stood out within the dream?

Dream Interpretation:

Fulfillment Date of Dream: _____

Dream

Ecclesiastes 10:14 (ESV)

A fool multiplies words, though no man knows what is to be, and who can tell him what will be after him?

Date: _____

What did you dream?

_____
_____
_____
_____
_____
_____
_____
_____
_____
_____
_____
_____
_____
_____
_____
_____

What stood out within the dream?

Dream Interpretation:

Fulfillment Date of Dream: _____

Dream

2 Kings 17:6 (ESV)

In the ninth year of Hoshea, the king of Assyria captured Samaria, and he carried the Israelites away to Assyria and placed them in Halah, and on the Habor, the river of Gozan, and in the cities of the Medes.

Date: _____

What did you dream?

_____
_____
_____
_____
_____
_____
_____
_____
_____
_____
_____
_____
_____
_____

What stood out within the dream?

Dream Interpretation:

Fulfillment Date of Dream: _____

Dream

Psalm 25:3 (ESV)

Indeed, none who wait for you shall be put to shame; they shall be ashamed who are wantonly treacherous.

Date: _____

What did you dream?

_____
_____
_____
_____
_____
_____
_____
_____
_____
_____
_____
_____
_____
_____
_____

Dreams – Visions – God Said

What stood out within the dream?

Dream Interpretation:

Fulfillment Date of Dream: _____

Dream

Psalm 60:3 (ESV)

You have made your people see hard things; you have given us wine to drink that made us stagger.

Date: _____

What did you dream?

_____
_____
_____
_____
_____
_____
_____
_____
_____
_____
_____
_____
_____
_____
_____

Dreams – Visions – God Said

What stood out within the dream?

Dream Interpretation:

Fulfillment Date of Dream: _____

Dream

Psalm 119:158 (ESV)

I look at the faithless with disgust, because they do not keep your commands.

Date: _____

What did you dream?

_____
_____
_____
_____
_____
_____
_____
_____
_____
_____
_____
_____
_____
_____
_____

What stood out within the dream?

Dream Interpretation:

Fulfillment Date of Dream: _____

Dream

Isaiah 22:6 (ESV)

And Elam bore the quiver with chariots and horsemen, and Kir uncovered the shield.

Date: _____

What did you dream?

_____
_____
_____
_____
_____
_____
_____
_____
_____
_____
_____
_____
_____
_____

Dreams – Visions – God Said

What stood out within the dream?

_____

_____

_____

_____

Dream Interpretation:

_____

_____

_____

_____

_____

_____

_____

_____

_____

_____

_____

_____

_____

_____

_____

_____

_____

Fulfillment Date of Dream: _____

Dream

Isaiah 24:16 (ESV)

From the ends of the earth we hear songs of praise, of glory to the Righteous One. But I say, "I waste away, I waste away. Woe is me! For the traitors have betrayed, with betrayal the traitors have betrayed."

Date: _____

What did you dream?

_____
_____
_____
_____
_____
_____
_____
_____
_____
_____
_____
_____

What stood out within the dream?

Dream Interpretation:

Fulfillment Date of Dream: _____

Dream

Isaiah 33:1 (ESV)

Ah, you destroyer, who yourself have not been destroyed, you traitor, whom none has betrayed! When you have ceased to destroy, you will be destroyed; and when you have finished betraying, they will betray you.

Date: _____

What did you dream?

_____
_____
_____
_____
_____
_____
_____
_____
_____
_____
_____
_____

Dreams – Visions – God Said

What stood out within the dream?

Dream Interpretation:

Fulfillment Date of Dream: _____

Dream

Jeremiah 49:34 (ESV)

The word of the Lord that came to Jeremiah the prophet concerning Elam, in the beginning of the reign of Zedekiah king of Judah.

Date: _____

What did you dream?

_____
_____
_____
_____
_____
_____
_____
_____
_____
_____
_____
_____
_____
_____
_____

What stood out within the dream?

Dream Interpretation:

Fulfillment Date of Dream: _____

Dream

Daniel 5:9 (ESV)

Then King Belshazzar was greatly alarmed, and his color changed, and his lords were perplexed.

Date: _____

What did you dream?

_____
_____
_____
_____
_____
_____
_____
_____
_____
_____
_____
_____
_____
_____
_____

What stood out within the dream?

Dream Interpretation:

Fulfillment Date of Dream: _____

Dream

Daniel 5:28 (ESV)

Peres, your kingdom is divided and given to the Medes and Persians."

Date: _____

What did you dream?

_____
_____
_____
_____
_____
_____
_____
_____
_____
_____
_____
_____
_____
_____
_____
_____
_____
_____

What stood out within the dream?

Dream Interpretation:

Fulfillment Date of Dream: _____

Dream

1 Corinthians 14:6 (ESV)

Now, brothers, [a] if I come to you speaking in tongues, how will I benefit you unless I bring you some revelation or knowledge or prophecy or teaching?

Date: _____

What did you dream?

_____
_____
_____
_____
_____
_____
_____
_____
_____
_____
_____
_____
_____
_____

Dreams – Visions – God Said

What stood out within the dream?

Dream Interpretation:

Fulfillment Date of Dream: _____

Dream

2 Corinthians 11:16 (ESV)

I repeat, let no one think me foolish. But even if you do, accept me as a fool, so that I too may boast a little.

Date: _____

What did you dream?

_____
_____
_____
_____
_____
_____
_____
_____
_____
_____
_____
_____
_____
_____

What stood out within the dream?

Dream Interpretation:

Fulfillment Date of Dream: _____

Dream

2 Corinthians 11:18 (ESV)

Since many boast according to the flesh, I too will boast.

Date: _____

What did you dream?

_____
_____
_____
_____
_____
_____
_____
_____
_____
_____
_____
_____
_____
_____
_____
_____
_____

What stood out within the dream?

Dream Interpretation:

Fulfillment Date of Dream: _____

Dream

2 Corinthians 12:5 (ESV)

On behalf of this man I will boast, but on my own behalf I will not boast, except of my weaknesses.

Date: _____

What did you dream?

_____
_____
_____
_____
_____
_____
_____
_____
_____
_____
_____
_____
_____
_____

What stood out within the dream?

Dream Interpretation:

Fulfillment Date of Dream: _____

Dream

2 Corinthians 12:7 (ESV)

So to keep me from becoming conceited because of the surpassing greatness of the revelations, [a] a thorn was given me in the flesh, a messenger of Satan to harass me, to keep me from becoming conceited.

Date: _____

What did you dream?

_____
_____
_____
_____
_____
_____
_____
_____
_____
_____
_____
_____

What stood out within the dream?

Dream Interpretation:

Fulfillment Date of Dream: _____

Dream

2 Corinthians 12:9 (ESV)

But he said to me, "My grace is sufficient for you, for my power is made perfect in weakness." Therefore, I will boast all the more gladly of my weaknesses, so that the power of Christ may rest upon me.

Date: _____

What did you dream?

_____
_____
_____
_____
_____
_____
_____
_____
_____
_____
_____
_____
_____
_____

Dreams – Visions – God Said

What stood out within the dream?

_____

_____

_____

_____

Dream Interpretation:

_____

_____

_____

_____

_____

_____

_____

_____

_____

_____

_____

_____

_____

_____

_____

_____

Fulfillment Date of Dream: _____

Dream

Galatians 1:12 (ESV)

For I did not receive it from any man, nor was I taught it, but I received it through a revelation of Jesus Christ.

Date: _____

What did you dream?

_____
_____
_____
_____
_____
_____
_____
_____
_____
_____
_____
_____
_____
_____

What stood out within the dream?

Dream Interpretation:

Fulfillment Date of Dream: _____

Dream

Galatians 2:2 (ESV)

I went up because of a revelation and set before them (though privately before those who seemed influential) the gospel that I proclaim among the Gentiles, in order to make sure I was not running or had not run in vain.

Date: _____

What did you dream?

_____
_____
_____
_____
_____
_____
_____
_____
_____
_____
_____
_____
_____
_____
_____

What stood out within the dream?

_____

_____

_____

_____

Dream Interpretation:

_____

_____

_____

_____

_____

_____

_____

_____

_____

_____

_____

_____

_____

_____

_____

Fulfillment Date of Dream: _____

Dream

Ephesians 3:3 (ESV)

how the mystery was made known to me by revelation, as I have written briefly.

Date: _____

What did you dream?

_____
_____
_____
_____
_____
_____
_____
_____
_____
_____
_____
_____
_____
_____
_____

What stood out within the dream?

Dream Interpretation:

Fulfillment Date of Dream: _____

Dream

1 Thessalonians 4:15 (ESV)

For this we declare to you by a word from the Lord,[a] that we who are alive, who are left until the coming of the Lord, will not precede those who have fallen asleep.

Date: _____

What did you dream?

_____
_____
_____
_____
_____
_____
_____
_____
_____
_____
_____
_____
_____

What stood out within the dream?

Dream Interpretation:

Fulfillment Date of Dream: _____

Dream

Job 3:26 (ESV)

I am not at ease, nor am I quiet; I have no rest, but trouble comes."

Date: _____

What did you dream?

_____
_____
_____
_____
_____
_____
_____
_____
_____
_____
_____
_____
_____
_____
_____
_____

What stood out within the dream?

Dream Interpretation:

Fulfillment Date of Dream: _____

Dream

Job 7:4 (ESV)

When I lie down I say, 'When shall I arise?' But the night is long, and I am full of tossing till the dawn.

Date: _____

What did you dream?

_____
_____
_____
_____
_____
_____
_____
_____
_____
_____
_____
_____
_____
_____
_____
_____

What stood out within the dream?

___

Dream Interpretation:

___

Fulfillment Date of Dream: _____

Dream

Job 7:13 (ESV)

When I say, 'My bed will comfort me, my couch will ease my complaint,'

Date: _____

What did you dream?

_____
_____
_____
_____
_____
_____
_____
_____
_____
_____
_____
_____
_____
_____
_____
_____

What stood out within the dream?

Dream Interpretation:

Fulfillment Date of Dream: _____

Dream

Job 7:15 (ESV)

so that I would choose strangling and death rather than my bones.

Date: _____

What did you dream?

_____
_____
_____
_____
_____
_____
_____
_____
_____
_____
_____
_____
_____
_____
_____
_____

Dreams – Visions – God Said

What stood out within the dream?

_____

_____

_____

_____

Dream Interpretation:

_____

_____

_____

_____

_____

_____

_____

_____

_____

_____

_____

_____

_____

_____

_____

_____

Fulfillment Date of Dream: _____

Dream

Genesis 14:15 (ESV)

And he divided his forces against them by night, he and his servants, and defeated them and pursued them to Hobah, north of Damascus.

Date: _____

What did you dream?

_____
_____
_____
_____
_____
_____
_____
_____
_____
_____
_____
_____
_____
_____
_____
_____
_____

What stood out within the dream?

___

Dream Interpretation:

___

Fulfillment Date of Dream: _____

Dream

Acts 9:9 (ESV)

And for three days he was without sight, and neither ate nor drank.

Date: _____

What did you dream?

_____
_____
_____
_____
_____
_____
_____
_____
_____
_____
_____
_____
_____
_____
_____
_____
_____
_____

Dreams – Visions – God Said

What stood out within the dream?

Dream Interpretation:

Fulfillment Date of Dream: _____

Dream

Acts 10:3 (ESV)

About the ninth hour of the day[a] he saw clearly in a vision an angel of God come in and say to him, "Cornelius."

Date: _____

What did you dream?

_____
_____
_____
_____
_____
_____
_____
_____
_____
_____
_____
_____
_____
_____
_____
_____

What stood out within the dream?

Dreams – Visions – God Said

_____
_____
_____
_____

Dream Interpretation:

_____
_____
_____
_____
_____
_____
_____
_____
_____
_____
_____
_____
_____
_____
_____
_____
_____
_____
_____
_____

Fulfillment Date of Dream: _____

Dream

Acts 10:17 (ESV)

Now while Peter was inwardly perplexed as to what the vision that he had seen might mean, behold, the men who were sent by Cornelius, having made inquiry for Simon's house, stood at the gate.

Date: _____

What did you dream?

_____
_____
_____
_____
_____
_____
_____
_____
_____
_____
_____
_____
_____
_____
_____
_____
_____

What stood out within the dream?

Dream Interpretation:

Fulfillment Date of Dream: _____

Dream

Acts 11:5 (ESV)

" I was in the city of Joppa praying, and in a trance I saw a vision, something like a great sheet descending, being let down from heaven by its four corners, and it came down to me.

Date: _____

What did you dream?

_____
_____
_____
_____
_____
_____
_____
_____
_____
_____
_____
_____
_____

Dreams – Visions – God Said

What stood out within the dream?

Dream Interpretation:

Fulfillment Date of Dream: _____

Dream

Acts 12:9 (ESV)

And he went out and followed him. He did not know that what was being done by the angel was real, but thought he was seeing a vision.

Date: _____

What did you dream?

_____
_____
_____
_____
_____
_____
_____
_____
_____
_____
_____
_____
_____
_____
_____

What stood out within the dream?

Dream Interpretation:

Fulfillment Date of Dream: _____

Dream

Acts 16:9 (ESV)

And a vision appeared to Paul in the night: a man of Macedonia was standing there, urging him and saying, "Come over to Macedonia and help us."

Date: _____

What did you dream?

_____
_____
_____
_____
_____
_____
_____
_____
_____
_____
_____
_____
_____
_____
_____

Dreams – Visions – God Said

What stood out within the dream?

_____

_____

_____

_____

Dream Interpretation:

_____

_____

_____

_____

_____

_____

_____

_____

_____

_____

_____

_____

_____

_____

_____

Fulfillment Date of Dream: _____

Dream

Acts 16:10 (ESV)

And when Paul[a] had seen the vision, immediately we sought to go on into Macedonia, concluding that God had called us to preach the gospel to them.

Date: _____

What did you dream?

_____
_____
_____
_____
_____
_____
_____
_____
_____
_____
_____
_____
_____
_____
_____
_____

What stood out within the dream?

Dream Interpretation:

Fulfillment Date of Dream: _____

Dream

Acts 18:9 (ESV)

And the Lord said to Paul one night in a vision, "Do not be afraid, but go on speaking and do not be silent,

Date: _____

What did you dream?

_____
_____
_____
_____
_____
_____
_____
_____
_____
_____
_____
_____
_____
_____

What stood out within the dream?

Dream Interpretation:

Fulfillment Date of Dream: _____

Dream

Acts 22:12 (ESV)

And one Ananias, a devout man according to the law, well-spoken of by all the Jews who lived there,

Date: _____

What did you dream?

_____
_____
_____
_____
_____
_____
_____
_____
_____
_____
_____
_____
_____
_____

What stood out within the dream?

Dream Interpretation:

Fulfillment Date of Dream: _____

Dream

2 Corinthians 11:32 (ESV)

At Damascus, the governor under King Aretas was guarding the city of Damascus in order to seize me,

Date: _____

What did you dream?

_____
_____
_____
_____
_____
_____
_____
_____
_____
_____
_____
_____
_____
_____
_____

What stood out within the dream?

_____
_____
_____
_____

Dream Interpretation:

_____
_____
_____
_____
_____
_____
_____
_____
_____
_____
_____
_____
_____
_____
_____
_____
_____

Fulfillment Date of Dream: _____

Dream

Galatians 1:17 (ESV)

nor did I go up to Jerusalem to those who were apostles before me, but I went away into Arabia, and returned again to Damascus.

Date: _____

What did you dream?

_____
_____
_____
_____
_____
_____
_____
_____
_____
_____
_____
_____
_____
_____
_____

What stood out within the dream?

Dream Interpretation:

Fulfillment Date of Dream: _____

Dream

2 Peter 3:4 (ESV)

"They will say, "Where is the promise of his coming? For ever since the fathers fell asleep, all things are continuing as they were from the beginning of creation."

Date: _____

What did you dream?

_____
_____
_____
_____
_____
_____
_____
_____
_____
_____
_____
_____
_____
_____
_____
_____

What stood out within the dream?

_____

_____

_____

_____

Dream Interpretation:

_____

_____

_____

_____

_____

_____

_____

_____

_____

_____

_____

_____

_____

_____

_____

Fulfillment Date of Dream: _____

Dream

Isaiah 5:19 (ESV)

who say: "Let him be quick, Let him speed his work that we may see it;

let the counsel of the Holy One of Israel draw near, and let it come, that we may know it!"

Date: _____

What did you dream?

_____
_____
_____
_____
_____
_____
_____
_____
_____
_____
_____
_____

Dreams – Visions – God Said

What stood out within the dream?

Dream Interpretation:

Fulfillment Date of Dream: _____

Dream

Jeremiah 5:12 (ESV)

They have spoken falsely of the Lord and have said, 'He will do nothing; no disaster will come upon us, nor shall we see sword or famine

Date: _____

What did you dream?

_____
_____
_____
_____
_____
_____
_____
_____
_____
_____
_____
_____
_____
_____
_____

Dreams – Visions – God Said

What stood out within the dream?

Dream Interpretation:

Fulfillment Date of Dream: _____

Dream

Ezekiel 7:26 (ESV)

Disaster comes upon disaster; rumor follows rumor. They seek a vision from the prophet, while the law[a] perishes from the priest and counsel from the elders.

Date: _____

What did you dream?

_____
_____
_____
_____
_____
_____
_____
_____
_____
_____
_____
_____
_____
_____
_____
_____

What stood out within the dream?

_____

_____

_____

_____

Dream Interpretation:

_____

_____

_____

_____

_____

_____

_____

_____

_____

_____

_____

_____

_____

_____

_____

Fulfillment Date of Dream: _____

Dream

Ezekiel 11:3 (ESV)

who say, 'The time is not near[a] to build houses. This city is the cauldron, and we are the meat.'

Date: _____

What did you dream?

_____
_____
_____
_____
_____
_____
_____
_____
_____
_____
_____
_____
_____
_____
_____
_____
_____

What stood out within the dream?

Dream Interpretation:

Fulfillment Date of Dream: _____

Dream

Ezekiel 12:21 (ESV)

And the word of the Lord came to me:

Date: _____

What did you dream?

_____
_____
_____
_____
_____
_____
_____
_____
_____
_____
_____
_____
_____
_____
_____
_____
_____

Dreams – Visions – God Said

What stood out within the dream?

_____

_____

_____

_____

Dream Interpretation:

_____

_____

_____

_____

_____

_____

_____

_____

_____

_____

_____

_____

_____

_____

_____

_____

_____

Fulfillment Date of Dream: _____

Dream

Ezekiel 12:27 (ESV)

" "Son of man, behold, they of the house of Israel say, 'The vision that he sees is for many days from now, and he prophesies of times far off.'

Date: _____

What did you dream?

_____
_____
_____
_____
_____
_____
_____
_____
_____
_____
_____
_____
_____
_____
_____

Dreams – Visions – God Said

What stood out within the dream?

Dream Interpretation:

Fulfillment Date of Dream: _____

Dream

Ezekiel 16:44 (ESV)

"Behold, everyone who uses proverbs will use this proverb about you: 'Like mother, like daughter.'

Date: _____

What did you dream?

_____
_____
_____
_____
_____
_____
_____
_____
_____
_____
_____
_____
_____
_____
_____

What stood out within the dream?

Dream Interpretation:

Fulfillment Date of Dream: _____

Dream

Ezekiel 18:2 (ESV)

"What do you[a] mean by repeating this proverb concerning the land of Israel, 'The fathers have eaten sour grapes, and the children's teeth are set on edge'?

Date: _____

What did you dream?

_____
_____
_____
_____
_____
_____
_____
_____
_____
_____
_____
_____
_____
_____

_____

_____

What stood out within the dream?

_____

_____

_____

_____

Dream Interpretation:

_____

_____

_____

_____

_____

_____

_____

_____

_____

_____

_____

_____

_____

_____

Fulfillment Date of Dream: _____

Dream

Ezekiel 18:3 (ESV)

As I live, declares the Lord God, this proverb shall no more be used by you in Israel

Date: _____

What did you dream?

_____
_____
_____
_____
_____
_____
_____
_____
_____
_____
_____
_____
_____
_____
_____

Dreams – Visions – God Said

What stood out within the dream?

Dream Interpretation:

Fulfillment Date of Dream: _____

Dream

Amos 6:3 (ESV)

O you who put far away the day of disaster and bring near the seat of violence?

Date: _____

What did you dream?

_____
_____
_____
_____
_____
_____
_____
_____
_____
_____
_____
_____
_____
_____
_____
_____

What stood out within the dream?

_____
_____
_____
_____

Dream Interpretation:

_____
_____
_____
_____
_____
_____
_____
_____
_____
_____
_____
_____
_____
_____
_____
_____

Fulfillment Date of Dream: _____

Dream

Habakkuk 1:5 (ESV)

"Look among the nations, and see; wonder and be astounded. For I am doing a work in your days that you would not believe if told.

Date: _____

What did you dream?

_____
_____
_____
_____
_____
_____
_____
_____
_____
_____
_____
_____
_____
_____
_____
_____

What stood out within the dream?

Dream Interpretation:

Fulfillment Date of Dream: _____

Part Two

MY VISION

Fire

Dreams – Visions – God Said

My Vision

Joel 2:28 (ESV)

"And it shall come to pass afterward, that I will pour out my Spirit on all flesh; your sons and your daughters shall prophesy, your old men shall dream dreams, and your young men shall see visions.

Date: _____

Write the vision:

_____
_____
_____
_____
_____
_____
_____
_____
_____
_____
_____
_____
_____
_____

My Vision

What stood out within the vision?

Vision Interpretation:

Fulfillment Date of Vision: _____

My Vision

Joel 2:28 (ESV)

"And it shall come to pass afterward, that I will pour out my Spirit on all flesh; your sons and your daughters shall prophesy, your old men shall dream dreams, and your young men shall see visions.

Date: _____

Write the vision:

_____
_____
_____
_____
_____
_____
_____
_____
_____
_____
_____
_____
_____
_____

My Vision

What stood out within the vision?

Vision Interpretation:

Fulfillment Date of Vision: _____

My Vision

Joel 2:28 (ESV)

"And it shall come to pass afterward, that I will pour out my Spirit on all flesh; your sons and your daughters shall prophesy, your old men shall dream dreams, and your young men shall see visions.

Date: _____

Write the vision:

_____
_____
_____
_____
_____
_____
_____
_____
_____
_____
_____
_____
_____
_____
_____
_____

My Vision

What stood out within the vision?

Vision Interpretation:

Fulfillment Date of Vision: _____

My Vision

(Joel 2:28 ESV)

"And it shall come to pass afterward, that I will pour out my Spirit on all flesh; your sons and your daughters shall prophesy, your old men shall dream dreams, and your young men shall see visions.

Date: _____

Write the vision:

_____
_____
_____
_____
_____
_____
_____
_____
_____
_____
_____
_____
_____
_____
_____
_____

My Vision

What stood out within the vision?

_____
_____
_____
_____

Vision Interpretation:

_____
_____
_____
_____
_____
_____
_____
_____
_____
_____
_____
_____
_____
_____
_____
_____

Fulfillment Date of Vision: _____

My Vision

Joel 2:28 (ESV)

"And it shall come to pass afterward, that I will pour out my Spirit on all flesh; your sons and your daughters shall prophesy, your old men shall dream dreams, and your young men shall see visions.

Date: _____

Write the vision:

_____
_____
_____
_____
_____
_____
_____
_____
_____
_____
_____
_____
_____
_____
_____

My Vision

What stood out within the vision?

_____

_____

_____

_____

Vision Interpretation:

_____

_____

_____

_____

_____

_____

_____

_____

_____

_____

_____

_____

_____

_____

_____

_____

_____

Fulfillment Date of Vision: _____

My Vision

Joel 2:28 (ESV)

"And it shall come to pass afterward, that I will pour out my Spirit on all flesh; your sons and your daughters shall prophesy, your old men shall dream dreams, and your young men shall see visions.

Date: _____

Write the vision:

_____
_____
_____
_____
_____
_____
_____
_____
_____
_____
_____
_____
_____
_____
_____
_____

My Vision

What stood out within the vision?

Vision Interpretation:

Fulfillment Date of Vision: _____

My Vision

Joel 2:28 (ESV)

"And it shall come to pass afterward, that I will pour out my Spirit on all flesh; your sons and your daughters shall prophesy, your old men shall dream dreams, and your young men shall see visions.

Date: _____

Write the vision:

_____
_____
_____
_____
_____
_____
_____
_____
_____
_____
_____
_____
_____
_____
_____

My Vision

What stood out within the vision?

Vision Interpretation:

Fulfillment Date of Vision: _____

My Vision

Joel 2:28 (ESV)

"And it shall come to pass afterward, that I will pour out my Spirit on all flesh; your sons and your daughters shall prophesy, your old men shall dream dreams, and your young men shall see visions.

Date: _____

Write the vision:

_____
_____
_____
_____
_____
_____
_____
_____
_____
_____
_____
_____
_____
_____
_____

My Vision

What stood out within the vision?

_____

_____

_____

_____

Vision Interpretation:

_____

_____

_____

_____

_____

_____

_____

_____

_____

_____

_____

_____

_____

_____

_____

_____

Fulfillment Date of Vision: _____

My Vision

Joel 2:28 (ESV)

"And it shall come to pass afterward, that I will pour out my Spirit on all flesh; your sons and your daughters shall prophesy, your old men shall dream dreams, and your young men shall see visions.

Date: _____

Write the vision:

_____
_____
_____
_____
_____
_____
_____
_____
_____
_____
_____
_____
_____
_____

My Vision

_____

What stood out within the vision?

_____

_____

_____

_____

Vision Interpretation:

_____

_____

_____

_____

_____

_____

_____

_____

_____

_____

_____

_____

_____

_____

_____

_____

Fulfillment Date of Vision: _____

My Vision

Joel 2:28 (ESV)

"And it shall come to pass afterward, that I will pour out my Spirit on all flesh; your sons and your daughters shall prophesy, your old men shall dream dreams, and your young men shall see visions.

Date: _____

Write the vision:

_____

_____

_____

_____

_____

_____

_____

_____

_____

_____

_____

_____

_____

_____

My Vision

What stood out within the vision?

Vision Interpretation:

Fulfillment Date of Vision: _____

My Vision

Joel 2:28 (ESV)

"And it shall come to pass afterward, that I will pour out my Spirit on all flesh; your sons and your daughters shall prophesy, your old men shall dream dreams, and your young men shall see visions.

Date: _____

Write the vision:

_____
_____
_____
_____
_____
_____
_____
_____
_____
_____
_____
_____
_____
_____
_____

My Vision

What stood out within the vision?

Vision Interpretation:

Fulfillment Date of Vision: _____

My Vision

Joel 2:28 (ESV)

"And it shall come to pass afterward, that I will pour out my Spirit on all flesh; your sons and your daughters shall prophesy, your old men shall dream dreams, and your young men shall see visions.

Date: _____

Write the vision:

_____
_____
_____
_____
_____
_____
_____
_____
_____
_____
_____
_____
_____
_____
_____
_____

My Vision

What stood out within the vision?

_____

_____

_____

_____

Vision Interpretation:

_____

_____

_____

_____

_____

_____

_____

_____

_____

_____

_____

_____

_____

_____

_____

_____

Fulfillment Date of Vision: _____

DREAMS – VISIONS – GOD SAID

My Vision

Joel 2:28 (ESV)

"And it shall come to pass afterward, that I will pour out my Spirit on all flesh; your sons and your daughters shall prophesy, your old men shall dream dreams, and your young men shall see visions.

Date: _____

Write the vision:

_____
_____
_____
_____
_____
_____
_____
_____
_____
_____
_____
_____
_____
_____
_____
_____
_____

My Vision

What stood out within the vision?

_____
_____
_____
_____

Vision Interpretation:

_____
_____
_____
_____
_____
_____
_____
_____
_____
_____
_____
_____
_____
_____
_____
_____
_____

Fulfillment Date of Vision: _____

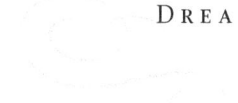

My Vision

Joel 2:28 (ESV)

"And it shall come to pass afterward, that I will pour out my Spirit on all flesh; your sons and your daughters shall prophesy, your old men shall dream dreams, and your young men shall see visions.

Date: _____

Write the vision:

_____

_____

_____

_____

_____

_____

_____

_____

_____

_____

_____

_____

_____

_____

My Vision

What stood out within the vision?

_____
_____
_____
_____

Vision Interpretation:

_____
_____
_____
_____
_____
_____
_____
_____
_____
_____
_____
_____
_____
_____
_____
_____
_____

Fulfillment Date of Vision: _____

My Vision

Joel 2:28 (ESV)

"And it shall come to pass afterward, that I will pour out my Spirit on all flesh; your sons and your daughters shall prophesy, your old men shall dream dreams, and your young men shall see visions.

Date: _____

Write the vision:

_____
_____
_____
_____
_____
_____
_____
_____
_____
_____
_____
_____
_____
_____
_____

My Vision

What stood out within the vision?

Vision Interpretation:

Fulfillment Date of Vision: _____

My Vision

Joel 2:28 (ESV)

"And it shall come to pass afterward, that I will pour out my Spirit on all flesh; your sons and your daughters shall prophesy, your old men shall dream dreams, and your young men shall see visions.

Date: _____

Write the vision:

_____
_____
_____
_____
_____
_____
_____
_____
_____
_____
_____
_____
_____
_____

My Vision

What stood out within the vision?

_____

_____

_____

_____

Vision Interpretation:

_____

_____

_____

_____

_____

_____

_____

_____

_____

_____

_____

_____

_____

_____

_____

Fulfillment Date of Vision: _____

My Vision

Joel 2:28 (ESV)

"And it shall come to pass afterward, that I will pour out my Spirit on all flesh; your sons and your daughters shall prophesy, your old men shall dream dreams, and your young men shall see visions.

Date: _____

Write the vision:

_____
_____
_____
_____
_____
_____
_____
_____
_____
_____
_____
_____
_____
_____
_____
_____

My Vision

What stood out within the vision?

Vision Interpretation:

Fulfillment Date of Vision: _____

My Vision

Joel 2:28 (ESV)

"And it shall come to pass afterward, that I will pour out my Spirit on all flesh; your sons and your daughters shall prophesy, your old men shall dream dreams, and your young men shall see visions.

Date: _____

Write the vision:

_____
_____
_____
_____
_____
_____
_____
_____
_____
_____
_____
_____
_____
_____
_____

My Vision

What stood out within the vision?

Vision Interpretation:

Fulfillment Date of Vision: _____

My Vision

Joel 2:28 (ESV)

"And it shall come to pass afterward, that I will pour out my Spirit on all flesh; your sons and your daughters shall prophesy, your old men shall dream dreams, and your young men shall see visions.

Date: _____

Write the vision:

_____
_____
_____
_____
_____
_____
_____
_____
_____
_____
_____
_____
_____
_____
_____

My Vision

What stood out within the vision?

_____

_____

_____

_____

Vision Interpretation:

_____

_____

_____

_____

_____

_____

_____

_____

_____

_____

_____

_____

_____

_____

_____

Fulfillment Date of Vision: _____

My Vision

Joel 2:28 (ESV)

"And it shall come to pass afterward, that I will pour out my Spirit on all flesh; your sons and your daughters shall prophesy, your old men shall dream dreams, and your young men shall see visions.

Date: _____

Write the vision:

_____
_____
_____
_____
_____
_____
_____
_____
_____
_____
_____
_____
_____
_____
_____

My Vision

What stood out within the vision?

Vision Interpretation:

Fulfillment Date of Vision: _____

Dreams – Visions – God Said

My Vision

Joel 2:28 (ESV)

"And it shall come to pass afterward, that I will pour out my Spirit on all flesh; your sons and your daughters shall prophesy, your old men shall dream dreams, and your young men shall see visions.

Date: _____

Write the vision:

_____
_____
_____
_____
_____
_____
_____
_____
_____
_____
_____
_____
_____
_____
_____

My Vision

What stood out within the vision?

_____

_____

_____

_____

Vision Interpretation:

_____

_____

_____

_____

_____

_____

_____

_____

_____

_____

_____

_____

_____

_____

_____

Fulfillment Date of Vision: _____

My Vision

Joel 2:28 (ESV)

"And it shall come to pass afterward, that I will pour out my Spirit on all flesh; your sons and your daughters shall prophesy, your old men shall dream dreams, and your young men shall see visions.

Date: _____

Write the vision:

_____
_____
_____
_____
_____
_____
_____
_____
_____
_____
_____
_____
_____
_____
_____

My Vision

What stood out within the vision?

_____
_____
_____
_____

Vision Interpretation:

_____
_____
_____
_____
_____
_____
_____
_____
_____
_____
_____
_____
_____
_____
_____
_____

Fulfillment Date of Vision: _____

My Vision

Joel 2:28 (ESV)

"And it shall come to pass afterward, that I will pour out my Spirit on all flesh; your sons and your daughters shall prophesy, your old men shall dream dreams, and your young men shall see visions.

Date: _____

Write the vision:

_____
_____
_____
_____
_____
_____
_____
_____
_____
_____
_____
_____
_____
_____

My Vision

What stood out within the vision?

_____

_____

_____

_____

Vision Interpretation:

_____

_____

_____

_____

_____

_____

_____

_____

_____

_____

_____

_____

_____

_____

_____

_____

Fulfillment Date of Vision: _____

My Vision

Joel 2:28 (ESV)

"And it shall come to pass afterward, that I will pour out my Spirit on all flesh; your sons and your daughters shall prophesy, your old men shall dream dreams, and your young men shall see visions.

Date: _____

Write the vision:

_____
_____
_____
_____
_____
_____
_____
_____
_____
_____
_____
_____
_____
_____
_____

My Vision

What stood out within the vision?

Vision Interpretation:

Fulfillment Date of Vision: _____

My Vision

Joel 2:28 (ESV)

"And it shall come to pass afterward, that I will pour out my Spirit on all flesh; your sons and your daughters shall prophesy, your old men shall dream dreams, and your young men shall see visions.

Date: _____

Write the vision:

_____
_____
_____
_____
_____
_____
_____
_____
_____
_____
_____
_____
_____
_____

My Vision

What stood out within the vision?

Vision Interpretation:

Fulfillment Date of Vision: _____

My Vision

Joel 2:28 (ESV)

"And it shall come to pass afterward, that I will pour out my Spirit on all flesh; your sons and your daughters shall prophesy, your old men shall dream dreams, and your young men shall see visions.

Date: _____

Write the vision:

_____
_____
_____
_____
_____
_____
_____
_____
_____
_____
_____
_____
_____
_____

My Vision

What stood out within the vision?

Vision Interpretation:

Fulfillment Date of Vision: _____

My Vision

Joel 2:28 (ESV)

"And it shall come to pass afterward, that I will pour out my Spirit on all flesh; your sons and your daughters shall prophesy, your old men shall dream dreams, and your young men shall see visions.

Date: _____

Write the vision:

_____

_____

_____

_____

_____

_____

_____

_____

_____

_____

_____

_____

_____

_____

_____

My Vision

What stood out within the vision?

Vision Interpretation:

Fulfillment Date of Vision: _____

My Vision

Joel 2:28 (ESV)

"And it shall come to pass afterward, that I will pour out my Spirit on all flesh; your sons and your daughters shall prophesy, your old men shall dream dreams, and your young men shall see visions.

Date: _____

Write the vision:

_____
_____
_____
_____
_____
_____
_____
_____
_____
_____
_____
_____
_____
_____
_____

What stood out within the vision?

_____

_____

_____

_____

Vision Interpretation:

_____

_____

_____

_____

_____

_____

_____

_____

_____

_____

_____

_____

_____

_____

_____

_____

Fulfillment Date of Vision: _____

My Vision

Joel 2:28 (ESV)

"And it shall come to pass afterward, that I will pour out my Spirit on all flesh; your sons and your daughters shall prophesy, your old men shall dream dreams, and your young men shall see visions.

Date: _____

Write the vision:

_____
_____
_____
_____
_____
_____
_____
_____
_____
_____
_____
_____
_____
_____
_____

My Vision

What stood out within the vision?

Vision Interpretation:

Fulfillment Date of Vision: _____

My Vision

Joel 2:28 (ESV)

"And it shall come to pass afterward, that I will pour out my Spirit on all flesh; your sons and your daughters shall prophesy, your old men shall dream dreams, and your young men shall see visions.

Date: _____

Write the vision:

_____
_____
_____
_____
_____
_____
_____
_____
_____
_____
_____
_____
_____
_____
_____

My Vision

What stood out within the vision?

_____

_____

_____

_____

Vision Interpretation:

_____

_____

_____

_____

_____

_____

_____

_____

_____

_____

_____

_____

_____

_____

_____

_____

Fulfillment Date of Vision: _____

My Vision

Joel 2:28 (ESV)

"And it shall come to pass afterward, that I will pour out my Spirit on all flesh; your sons and your daughters shall prophesy, your old men shall dream dreams, and your young men shall see visions.

Date: _____

Write the vision:

_____
_____
_____
_____
_____
_____
_____
_____
_____
_____
_____
_____
_____
_____
_____

My Vision

What stood out within the vision?

Vision Interpretation:

Fulfillment Date of Vision: _____

My Vision

Joel 2:28 (ESV)

"And it shall come to pass afterward, that I will pour out my Spirit on all flesh; your sons and your daughters shall prophesy, your old men shall dream dreams, and your young men shall see visions.

Date: _____

Write the vision:

_____
_____
_____
_____
_____
_____
_____
_____
_____
_____
_____
_____
_____
_____

My Vision

What stood out within the vision?

_____
_____
_____
_____

Vision Interpretation:

_____
_____
_____
_____
_____
_____
_____
_____
_____
_____
_____
_____
_____
_____
_____
_____
_____

Fulfillment Date of Vision: _____

My Vision

Joel 2:28 (ESV)

"And it shall come to pass afterward, that I will pour out my Spirit on all flesh; your sons and your daughters shall prophesy, your old men shall dream dreams, and your young men shall see visions.

Date: _____

Write the vision:

_____
_____
_____
_____
_____
_____
_____
_____
_____
_____
_____
_____
_____

My Vision

What stood out within the vision?

Vision Interpretation:

Fulfillment Date of Vision: _____

My Vision

Joel 2:28 (ESV)

"And it shall come to pass afterward, that I will pour out my Spirit on all flesh; your sons and your daughters shall prophesy, your old men shall dream dreams, and your young men shall see visions.

Date: _____

Write the vision:

_____
_____
_____
_____
_____
_____
_____
_____
_____
_____
_____
_____
_____
_____
_____

My Vision

What stood out within the vision?

Vision Interpretation:

Fulfillment Date of Vision: _____

My Vision

Joel 2:28 (ESV)

"And it shall come to pass afterward, that I will pour out my Spirit on all flesh; your sons and your daughters shall prophesy, your old men shall dream dreams, and your young men shall see visions.

Date: _____

Write the vision:

_____
_____
_____
_____
_____
_____
_____
_____
_____
_____
_____
_____
_____
_____

My Vision

What stood out within the vision?

Vision Interpretation:

Fulfillment Date of Vision: _____

My Vision

Joel 2:28 (ESV)

"And it shall come to pass afterward, that I will pour out my Spirit on all flesh; your sons and your daughters shall prophesy, your old men shall dream dreams, and your young men shall see visions.

Date: _____

Write the vision:

_____
_____
_____
_____
_____
_____
_____
_____
_____
_____
_____
_____
_____
_____
_____

My Vision

What stood out within the vision?

Vision Interpretation:

Fulfillment Date of Vision: _____

My Vision

Joel 2:28 (ESV)

"And it shall come to pass afterward, that I will pour out my Spirit on all flesh; your sons and your daughters shall prophesy, your old men shall dream dreams, and your young men shall see visions.

Date: _____

Write the vision:

_____
_____
_____
_____
_____
_____
_____
_____
_____
_____
_____
_____
_____
_____
_____

My Vision

What stood out within the vision?

Vision Interpretation:

Fulfillment Date of Vision: _____

My Vision

Joel 2:28 (ESV)

"And it shall come to pass afterward, that I will pour out my Spirit on all flesh; your sons and your daughters shall prophesy, your old men shall dream dreams, and your young men shall see visions.

Date: _____

Write the vision:

_____
_____
_____
_____
_____
_____
_____
_____
_____
_____
_____
_____
_____
_____
_____

My Vision

What stood out within the vision?

_____

_____

_____

_____

Vision Interpretation:

_____

_____

_____

_____

_____

_____

_____

_____

_____

_____

_____

_____

_____

_____

_____

_____

_____

Fulfillment Date of Vision: _____

My Vision

Joel 2:28 (ESV)

"And it shall come to pass afterward, that I will pour out my Spirit on all flesh; your sons and your daughters shall prophesy, your old men shall dream dreams, and your young men shall see visions.

Date: _____

Write the vision:

_____
_____
_____
_____
_____
_____
_____
_____
_____
_____
_____
_____
_____
_____
_____
_____
_____

My Vision

What stood out within the vision?

Vision Interpretation:

Fulfillment Date of Vision: _____

My Vision

Joel 2:28 (ESV)

"And it shall come to pass afterward, that I will pour out my Spirit on all flesh; your sons and your daughters shall prophesy, your old men shall dream dreams, and your young men shall see visions.

Date: _____

Write the vision:

_____

_____

_____

_____

_____

_____

_____

_____

_____

_____

_____

_____

_____

_____

_____

My Vision

What stood out within the vision?

_____

_____

_____

_____

Vision Interpretation:

_____

_____

_____

_____

_____

_____

_____

_____

_____

_____

_____

_____

_____

_____

_____

_____

Fulfillment Date of Vision: _____

Dreams – Visions – God Said

My Vision

Joel 2:28 (ESV)

"And it shall come to pass afterward, that I will pour out my Spirit on all flesh; your sons and your daughters shall prophesy, your old men shall dream dreams, and your young men shall see visions.

Date: _____

Write the vision:

_____
_____
_____
_____
_____
_____
_____
_____
_____
_____
_____
_____
_____
_____
_____
_____

My Vision

What stood out within the vision?

_____

_____

_____

_____

Vision Interpretation:

_____

_____

_____

_____

_____

_____

_____

_____

_____

_____

_____

_____

_____

_____

_____

_____

Fulfillment Date of Vision: _____

My Vision

Joel 2:28 (ESV)

"And it shall come to pass afterward, that I will pour out my Spirit on all flesh; your sons and your daughters shall prophesy, your old men shall dream dreams, and your young men shall see visions.

Date: _____

Write the vision:

_____
_____
_____
_____
_____
_____
_____
_____
_____
_____
_____
_____
_____
_____

My Vision

What stood out within the vision?

_____

_____

_____

_____

Vision Interpretation:

_____

_____

_____

_____

_____

_____

_____

_____

_____

_____

_____

_____

_____

_____

_____

_____

Fulfillment Date of Vision: _____

My Vision

Joel 2:28 (ESV)

"And it shall come to pass afterward, that I will pour out my Spirit on all flesh; your sons and your daughters shall prophesy, your old men shall dream dreams, and your young men shall see visions.

Date: _____

Write the vision:

_____
_____
_____
_____
_____
_____
_____
_____
_____
_____
_____
_____
_____
_____
_____
_____
_____
_____
_____
_____
_____
_____
_____
_____
_____

What stood out within the vision?

_____
_____
_____
_____

My Vision

Vision Interpretation:

_____
_____
_____
_____
_____
_____
_____
_____
_____
_____
_____
_____
_____
_____
_____
_____
_____
_____
_____
_____
_____

Fulfillment Date of Vision: _____

My Vision

Joel 2:28 (ESV)

"And it shall come to pass afterward, that I will pour out my Spirit on all flesh; your sons and your daughters shall prophesy, your old men shall dream dreams, and your young men shall see visions.

Date: _____

Write the vision:

_____

_____

_____

_____

_____

_____

_____

_____

_____

_____

_____

_____

_____

My Vision

What stood out within the vision?

_____

_____

_____

_____

Vision Interpretation:

_____

_____

_____

_____

_____

_____

_____

_____

_____

_____

_____

_____

_____

_____

_____

_____

Fulfillment Date of Vision: _____

My Vision

Joel 2:28 (ESV)

"And it shall come to pass afterward, that I will pour out my Spirit on all flesh; your sons and your daughters shall prophesy, your old men shall dream dreams, and your young men shall see visions.

Date: _____

Write the vision:

_____
_____
_____
_____
_____
_____
_____
_____
_____
_____
_____
_____
_____
_____

My Vision

What stood out within the vision?

_____
_____
_____
_____

Vision Interpretation:

_____
_____
_____
_____
_____
_____
_____
_____
_____
_____
_____
_____
_____
_____
_____
_____

Fulfillment Date of Vision: _____

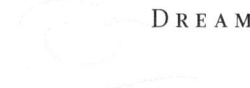

My Vision

Joel 2:28 (ESV)

"And it shall come to pass afterward, that I will pour out my Spirit on all flesh; your sons and your daughters shall prophesy, your old men shall dream dreams, and your young men shall see visions.

Date: _____

Write the vision:

_____
_____
_____
_____
_____
_____
_____
_____
_____
_____
_____
_____
_____
_____
_____

My Vision

What stood out within the vision?

_____
_____
_____
_____

Vision Interpretation:

_____
_____
_____
_____
_____
_____
_____
_____
_____
_____
_____
_____
_____
_____
_____
_____

Fulfillment Date of Vision: _____

My Vision

Joel 2:28 (ESV)

"And it shall come to pass afterward, that I will pour out my Spirit on all flesh; your sons and your daughters shall prophesy, your old men shall dream dreams, and your young men shall see visions.

Date: _____

Write the vision:

_____
_____
_____
_____
_____
_____
_____
_____
_____
_____
_____
_____
_____
_____

My Vision

What stood out within the vision?

_____
_____
_____
_____

Vision Interpretation:

_____
_____
_____
_____
_____
_____
_____
_____
_____
_____
_____
_____
_____
_____
_____
_____
_____

Fulfillment Date of Vision: _____

My Vision

Joel 2:28 (ESV)

"And it shall come to pass afterward, that I will pour out my Spirit on all flesh; your sons and your daughters shall prophesy, your old men shall dream dreams, and your young men shall see visions.

Date: _____

Write the vision:

_____
_____
_____
_____
_____
_____
_____
_____
_____
_____
_____
_____
_____
_____

My Vision

What stood out within the vision?

Vision Interpretation:

Fulfillment Date of Vision: _____

My Vision

Joel 2:28 (ESV)

"And it shall come to pass afterward, that I will pour out my Spirit on all flesh; your sons and your daughters shall prophesy, your old men shall dream dreams, and your young men shall see visions.

Date: _____

Write the vision:

_____
_____
_____
_____
_____
_____
_____
_____
_____
_____
_____
_____
_____
_____
_____

My Vision

What stood out within the vision?

_____

_____

_____

_____

Vision Interpretation:

_____

_____

_____

_____

_____

_____

_____

_____

_____

_____

_____

_____

_____

_____

_____

_____

_____

Fulfillment Date of Vision: _____

My Vision

Joel 2:28 (ESV)

"And it shall come to pass afterward, that I will pour out my Spirit on all flesh; your sons and your daughters shall prophesy, your old men shall dream dreams, and your young men shall see visions.

Date: _____

Write the vision:

_____
_____
_____
_____
_____
_____
_____
_____
_____
_____
_____
_____
_____
_____
_____

My Vision

What stood out within the vision?

_____

_____

_____

_____

Vision Interpretation:

_____

_____

_____

_____

_____

_____

_____

_____

_____

_____

_____

_____

_____

_____

_____

Fulfillment Date of Vision: _____

My Vision

Joel 2:28 (ESV)

"And it shall come to pass afterward, that I will pour out my Spirit on all flesh; your sons and your daughters shall prophesy, your old men shall dream dreams, and your young men shall see visions.

Date: _____

Write the vision:

_____
_____
_____
_____
_____
_____
_____
_____
_____
_____
_____
_____
_____
_____
_____

My Vision

What stood out within the vision?

Vision Interpretation:

Fulfillment Date of Vision: _____

My Vision

Joel 2:28 (ESV)

"And it shall come to pass afterward, that I will pour out my Spirit on all flesh; your sons and your daughters shall prophesy, your old men shall dream dreams, and your young men shall see visions.

Date: _____

Write the vision:

_____
_____
_____
_____
_____
_____
_____
_____
_____
_____
_____
_____
_____
_____

My Vision

What stood out within the vision?

Vision Interpretation:

Fulfillment Date of Vision: _____

My Vision

Joel 2:28 (ESV)

"And it shall come to pass afterward, that I will pour out my Spirit on all flesh; your sons and your daughters shall prophesy, your old men shall dream dreams, and your young men shall see visions.

Date: _____

Write the vision:

_____
_____
_____
_____
_____
_____
_____
_____
_____
_____
_____
_____
_____
_____
_____
_____

My Vision

What stood out within the vision?

_____

_____

_____

_____

Vision Interpretation:

_____

_____

_____

_____

_____

_____

_____

_____

_____

_____

_____

_____

_____

_____

_____

_____

Fulfillment Date of Vision: _____

My Vision

Joel 2:28 (ESV)

"And it shall come to pass afterward, that I will pour out my Spirit on all flesh; your sons and your daughters shall prophesy, your old men shall dream dreams, and your young men shall see visions.

Date: _____

Write the vision:

_____

_____

_____

_____

_____

_____

_____

_____

_____

_____

_____

_____

_____

_____

My Vision

What stood out within the vision?

_____

_____

_____

_____

Vision Interpretation:

_____

_____

_____

_____

_____

_____

_____

_____

_____

_____

_____

_____

_____

_____

_____

_____

Fulfillment Date of Vision: _____

My Vision

Joel 2:28 (ESV)

"And it shall come to pass afterward, that I will pour out my Spirit on all flesh; your sons and your daughters shall prophesy, your old men shall dream dreams, and your young men shall see visions.

Date: _____

Write the vision:

_____

_____

_____

_____

_____

_____

_____

_____

_____

_____

_____

_____

_____

_____

_____

My Vision

What stood out within the vision?

_____

_____

_____

_____

Vision Interpretation:

_____

_____

_____

_____

_____

_____

_____

_____

_____

_____

_____

_____

_____

_____

_____

_____

Fulfillment Date of Vision: _____

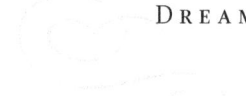

My Vision

Joel 2:28 (ESV)

"And it shall come to pass afterward, that I will pour out my Spirit on all flesh; your sons and your daughters shall prophesy, your old men shall dream dreams, and your young men shall see visions.

Date: _____

Write the vision:

_____
_____
_____
_____
_____
_____
_____
_____
_____
_____
_____
_____
_____
_____
_____

My Vision

What stood out within the vision?

_____

_____

_____

_____

Vision Interpretation:

_____

_____

_____

_____

_____

_____

_____

_____

_____

_____

_____

_____

_____

_____

_____

_____

_____

Fulfillment Date of Vision: _____

My Vision

Joel 2:28 (ESV)

"And it shall come to pass afterward, that I will pour out my Spirit on all flesh; your sons and your daughters shall prophesy, your old men shall dream dreams, and your young men shall see visions.

Date: _____

Write the vision:

_____
_____
_____
_____
_____
_____
_____
_____
_____
_____
_____
_____
_____
_____
_____
_____
_____
_____
_____
_____

_____

What stood out within the vision?

_____
_____
_____

My Vision

Vision Interpretation:

_____
_____
_____
_____
_____
_____
_____
_____
_____
_____
_____
_____
_____
_____
_____
_____
_____
_____
_____
_____
_____

Fulfillment Date of Vision: _____

My Vision

Joel 2:28 (ESV)

"And it shall come to pass afterward, that I will pour out my Spirit on all flesh; your sons and your daughters shall prophesy, your old men shall dream dreams, and your young men shall see visions.

Date: _____

Write the vision:

_____
_____
_____
_____
_____
_____
_____
_____
_____
_____
_____
_____
_____
_____
_____

My Vision

What stood out within the vision?

_____
_____
_____
_____

Vision Interpretation:

_____
_____
_____
_____
_____
_____
_____
_____
_____
_____
_____
_____
_____
_____
_____

Fulfillment Date of Vision: _____

Dreams – Visions – God Said

My Vision

Joel 2:28 (ESV)

"And it shall come to pass afterward, that I will pour out my Spirit on all flesh; your sons and your daughters shall prophesy, your old men shall dream dreams, and your young men shall see visions.

Date: _____

Write the vision:

_____
_____
_____
_____
_____
_____
_____
_____
_____
_____
_____
_____
_____
_____
_____
_____

My Vision

What stood out within the vision?

_____

_____

_____

_____

Vision Interpretation:

_____

_____

_____

_____

_____

_____

_____

_____

_____

_____

_____

_____

_____

_____

_____

_____

_____

Fulfillment Date of Vision: _____

My Vision

Joel 2:28 (ESV)

"And it shall come to pass afterward, that I will pour out my Spirit on all flesh; your sons and your daughters shall prophesy, your old men shall dream dreams, and your young men shall see visions.

Date: _____

Write the vision:

_____
_____
_____
_____
_____
_____
_____
_____
_____
_____
_____
_____

My Vision

What stood out within the vision?

_____

_____

_____

_____

Vision Interpretation:

_____

_____

_____

_____

_____

_____

_____

_____

_____

_____

_____

_____

_____

_____

_____

_____

Fulfillment Date of Vision: _____

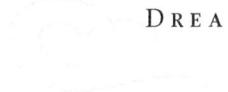

My Vision

Joel 2:28 (ESV)

"And it shall come to pass afterward, that I will pour out my Spirit on all flesh; your sons and your daughters shall prophesy, your old men shall dream dreams, and your young men shall see visions.

Date: _____

Write the vision:

_____
_____
_____
_____
_____
_____
_____
_____
_____
_____
_____
_____
_____
_____

My Vision

What stood out within the vision?

_____

_____

_____

_____

Vision Interpretation:

_____

_____

_____

_____

_____

_____

_____

_____

_____

_____

_____

_____

_____

_____

_____

_____

_____

Fulfillment Date of Vision: _____

My Vision

Joel 2:28 (ESV)

"And it shall come to pass afterward, that I will pour out my Spirit on all flesh; your sons and your daughters shall prophesy, your old men shall dream dreams, and your young men shall see visions.

Date: _____

Write the vision:

_____

_____

_____

_____

_____

_____

_____

_____

_____

_____

_____

_____

_____

_____

_____

My Vision

What stood out within the vision?

_____
_____
_____
_____

Vision Interpretation:

_____
_____
_____
_____
_____
_____
_____
_____
_____
_____
_____
_____
_____
_____
_____
_____

Fulfillment Date of Vision: _____

My Vision

Joel 2:28 (ESV)

"And it shall come to pass afterward, that I will pour out my Spirit on all flesh; your sons and your daughters shall prophesy, your old men shall dream dreams, and your young men shall see visions.

Date: _____

Write the vision:

_____
_____
_____
_____
_____
_____
_____
_____
_____
_____
_____
_____
_____
_____
_____

My Vision

What stood out within the vision?

_____

_____

_____

_____

Vision Interpretation:

_____

_____

_____

_____

_____

_____

_____

_____

_____

_____

_____

_____

_____

_____

_____

_____

Fulfillment Date of Vision: _____

My Vision

Joel 2:28 (ESV)

"And it shall come to pass afterward, that I will pour out my Spirit on all flesh; your sons and your daughters shall prophesy, your old men shall dream dreams, and your young men shall see visions.

Date: _____

Write the vision:

_____
_____
_____
_____
_____
_____
_____
_____
_____
_____
_____
_____
_____
_____
_____
_____

My Vision

What stood out within the vision?

_____

_____

_____

_____

Vision Interpretation:

_____

_____

_____

_____

_____

_____

_____

_____

_____

_____

_____

_____

_____

_____

_____

_____

Fulfillment Date of Vision: _____

My Vision

Joel 2:28 (ESV)

"And it shall come to pass afterward, that I will pour out my Spirit on all flesh; your sons and your daughters shall prophesy, your old men shall dream dreams, and your young men shall see visions.

Date: _____

Write the vision:

_____
_____
_____
_____
_____
_____
_____
_____
_____
_____
_____
_____
_____
_____
_____

My Vision

What stood out within the vision?

_____
_____
_____
_____

Vision Interpretation:

_____
_____
_____
_____
_____
_____
_____
_____
_____
_____
_____
_____
_____
_____
_____
_____
_____

Fulfillment Date of Vision: _____

My Vision

Joel 2:28 (ESV)

"And it shall come to pass afterward, that I will pour out my Spirit on all flesh; your sons and your daughters shall prophesy, your old men shall dream dreams, and your young men shall see visions.

Date: _____

Write the vision:

_____

_____

_____

_____

_____

_____

_____

_____

_____

_____

_____

_____

_____

_____

My Vision

What stood out within the vision?

_____

_____

_____

_____

Vision Interpretation:

_____

_____

_____

_____

_____

_____

_____

_____

_____

_____

_____

_____

_____

_____

_____

_____

_____

Fulfillment Date of Vision: _____

My Vision

Joel 2:28 (ESV)

"And it shall come to pass afterward, that I will pour out my Spirit on all flesh; your sons and your daughters shall prophesy, your old men shall dream dreams, and your young men shall see visions.

Date: _____

Write the vision:

_____

_____

_____

_____

_____

_____

_____

_____

_____

_____

_____

_____

_____

_____

_____

_____

_____

_____

My Vision

What stood out within the vision?

_____

_____

_____

_____

Vision Interpretation:

_____

_____

_____

_____

_____

_____

_____

_____

_____

_____

_____

_____

_____

_____

_____

_____

Fulfillment Date of Vision: _____

My Vision

Joel 2:28 (ESV)

"And it shall come to pass afterward, that I will pour out my Spirit on all flesh; your sons and your daughters shall prophesy, your old men shall dream dreams, and your young men shall see visions.

Date: _____

Write the vision:

_____
_____
_____
_____
_____
_____
_____
_____
_____
_____
_____
_____
_____
_____

My Vision

What stood out within the vision?

_____

_____

_____

_____

Vision Interpretation:

_____

_____

_____

_____

_____

_____

_____

_____

_____

_____

_____

_____

_____

_____

_____

_____

Fulfillment Date of Vision: _____

My Vision

Joel 2:28 (ESV)

"And it shall come to pass afterward, that I will pour out my Spirit on all flesh; your sons and your daughters shall prophesy, your old men shall dream dreams, and your young men shall see visions.

Date: _____

Write the vision:

_____
_____
_____
_____
_____
_____
_____
_____
_____
_____
_____
_____
_____
_____
_____
_____

My Vision

What stood out within the vision?

Vision Interpretation:

Fulfillment Date of Vision: _____

My Vision

Joel 2:28 (ESV)

"And it shall come to pass afterward, that I will pour out my Spirit on all flesh; your sons and your daughters shall prophesy, your old men shall dream dreams, and your young men shall see visions.

Date: _____

Write the vision:

_____
_____
_____
_____
_____
_____
_____
_____
_____
_____
_____
_____
_____
_____
_____
_____

My Vision

What stood out within the vision?

_____

_____

_____

_____

Vision Interpretation:

_____

_____

_____

_____

_____

_____

_____

_____

_____

_____

_____

_____

_____

_____

_____

Fulfillment Date of Vision: _____

My Vision

Joel 2:28 (ESV)

"And it shall come to pass afterward, that I will pour out my Spirit on all flesh; your sons and your daughters shall prophesy, your old men shall dream dreams, and your young men shall see visions.

Date: _____

Write the vision:

_____
_____
_____
_____
_____
_____
_____
_____
_____
_____
_____
_____
_____

My Vision

What stood out within the vision?

Vision Interpretation:

Fulfillment Date of Vision: _____

My Vision

Joel 2:28 (ESV)

"And it shall come to pass afterward, that I will pour out my Spirit on all flesh; your sons and your daughters shall prophesy, your old men shall dream dreams, and your young men shall see visions.

Date: _____

Write the vision:

_____
_____
_____
_____
_____
_____
_____
_____
_____
_____
_____
_____
_____
_____
_____
_____

My Vision

What stood out within the vision?

_____
_____
_____
_____

Vision Interpretation:

_____
_____
_____
_____
_____
_____
_____
_____
_____
_____
_____
_____
_____
_____
_____
_____
_____

Fulfillment Date of Vision: _____

Dreams – Visions – God Said

My Vision

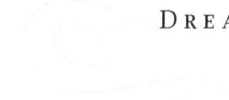

Joel 2:28 (ESV)

"And it shall come to pass afterward, that I will pour out my Spirit on all flesh; your sons and your daughters shall prophesy, your old men shall dream dreams, and your young men shall see visions.

Date: _____

Write the vision:

_____

_____

_____

_____

_____

_____

_____

_____

_____

_____

_____

_____

_____

_____

My Vision

What stood out within the vision?

Vision Interpretation:

Fulfillment Date of Vision: _____

My Vision

Joel 2:28 (ESV)

"And it shall come to pass afterward, that I will pour out my Spirit on all flesh; your sons and your daughters shall prophesy, your old men shall dream dreams, and your young men shall see visions.

Date: _____

Write the vision:

_____
_____
_____
_____
_____
_____
_____
_____
_____
_____
_____
_____
_____

My Vision

What stood out within the vision?

_____

_____

_____

_____

Vision Interpretation:

_____

_____

_____

_____

_____

_____

_____

_____

_____

_____

_____

_____

_____

_____

_____

Fulfillment Date of Vision: _____

My Vision

Joel 2:28 (ESV)

"And it shall come to pass afterward, that I will pour out my Spirit on all flesh; your sons and your daughters shall prophesy, your old men shall dream dreams, and your young men shall see visions.

Date: _____

Write the vision:

_____
_____
_____
_____
_____
_____
_____
_____
_____
_____
_____
_____
_____
_____
_____

My Vision

What stood out within the vision?

_____

_____

_____

_____

Vision Interpretation:

_____

_____

_____

_____

_____

_____

_____

_____

_____

_____

_____

_____

_____

_____

_____

_____

Fulfillment Date of Vision: _____

My Vision

Joel 2:28 (ESV)

"And it shall come to pass afterward, that I will pour out my Spirit on all flesh; your sons and your daughters shall prophesy, your old men shall dream dreams, and your young men shall see visions.

Date: _____

Write the vision:

_____
_____
_____
_____
_____
_____
_____
_____
_____
_____
_____
_____
_____
_____

My Vision

What stood out within the vision?

_____
_____
_____
_____

Vision Interpretation:

_____
_____
_____
_____
_____
_____
_____
_____
_____
_____
_____
_____
_____
_____
_____
_____

Fulfillment Date of Vision: _____

My Vision

Joel 2:28 (ESV)

"And it shall come to pass afterward, that I will pour out my Spirit on all flesh; your sons and your daughters shall prophesy, your old men shall dream dreams, and your young men shall see visions.

Date: _____

Write the vision:

_____
_____
_____
_____
_____
_____
_____
_____
_____
_____
_____
_____
_____
_____
_____

My Vision

What stood out within the vision?

Vision Interpretation:

Fulfillment Date of Vision: _____

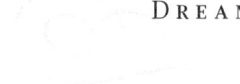

My Vision

Joel 2:28 (ESV)

"And it shall come to pass afterward, that I will pour out my Spirit on all flesh; your sons and your daughters shall prophesy, your old men shall dream dreams, and your young men shall see visions.

Date: _____

Write the vision:

_____
_____
_____
_____
_____
_____
_____
_____
_____
_____
_____
_____
_____
_____
_____
_____

My Vision

What stood out within the vision?

Vision Interpretation:

Fulfillment Date of Vision: _____

My Vision

Joel 2:28 (ESV)

"And it shall come to pass afterward, that I will pour out my Spirit on all flesh; your sons and your daughters shall prophesy, your old men shall dream dreams, and your young men shall see visions.

Date: _____

Write the vision:

_____
_____
_____
_____
_____
_____
_____
_____
_____
_____
_____
_____
_____
_____
_____
_____

My Vision

What stood out within the vision?

Vision Interpretation:

Fulfillment Date of Vision: _____

My Vision

Joel 2:28 (ESV)

"And it shall come to pass afterward, that I will pour out my Spirit on all flesh; your sons and your daughters shall prophesy, your old men shall dream dreams, and your young men shall see visions.

Date: _____

Write the vision:

_____
_____
_____
_____
_____
_____
_____
_____
_____
_____
_____
_____
_____
_____

My Vision

What stood out within the vision?

_____

_____

_____

_____

Vision Interpretation:

_____

_____

_____

_____

_____

_____

_____

_____

_____

_____

_____

_____

_____

_____

_____

_____

Fulfillment Date of Vision: _____

My Vision

Joel 2:28 (ESV)

"And it shall come to pass afterward, that I will pour out my Spirit on all flesh; your sons and your daughters shall prophesy, your old men shall dream dreams, and your young men shall see visions.

Date: _____

Write the vision:

_____
_____
_____
_____
_____
_____
_____
_____
_____
_____
_____
_____
_____
_____

My Vision

What stood out within the vision?

Vision Interpretation:

Fulfillment Date of Vision: _____

My Vision

Joel 2:28 (ESV)

"And it shall come to pass afterward, that I will pour out my Spirit on all flesh; your sons and your daughters shall prophesy, your old men shall dream dreams, and your young men shall see visions.

Date: _____

Write the vision:

_____
_____
_____
_____
_____
_____
_____
_____
_____
_____
_____
_____
_____
_____

My Vision

What stood out within the vision?

Vision Interpretation:

Fulfillment Date of Vision: _____

My Vision

Joel 2:28 (ESV)

"And it shall come to pass afterward, that I will pour out my Spirit on all flesh; your sons and your daughters shall prophesy, your old men shall dream dreams, and your young men shall see visions.

Date: _____

Write the vision:

_____
_____
_____
_____
_____
_____
_____
_____
_____
_____
_____
_____
_____
_____

My Vision

What stood out within the vision?

_____
_____
_____
_____

Vision Interpretation:

_____
_____
_____
_____
_____
_____
_____
_____
_____
_____
_____
_____
_____
_____
_____
_____
_____

Fulfillment Date of Vision: _____

My Vision

Joel 2:28 (ESV)

"And it shall come to pass afterward, that I will pour out my Spirit on all flesh; your sons and your daughters shall prophesy, your old men shall dream dreams, and your young men shall see visions.

Date: _____

Write the vision:

_____
_____
_____
_____
_____
_____
_____
_____
_____
_____
_____
_____
_____
_____
_____

My Vision

What stood out within the vision?

_____

_____

_____

_____

Vision Interpretation:

_____

_____

_____

_____

_____

_____

_____

_____

_____

_____

_____

_____

_____

_____

_____

Fulfillment Date of Vision: _____

My Vision

Joel 2:28 (ESV)

"And it shall come to pass afterward, that I will pour out my Spirit on all flesh; your sons and your daughters shall prophesy, your old men shall dream dreams, and your young men shall see visions.

Date: _____

Write the vision:

_____
_____
_____
_____
_____
_____
_____
_____
_____
_____
_____
_____
_____
_____

My Vision

What stood out within the vision?

_____

_____

_____

_____

Vision Interpretation:

_____

_____

_____

_____

_____

_____

_____

_____

_____

_____

_____

_____

_____

_____

_____

_____

_____

Fulfillment Date of Vision: _____

My Vision

Joel 2:28 (ESV)

"And it shall come to pass afterward, that I will pour out my Spirit on all flesh; your sons and your daughters shall prophesy, your old men shall dream dreams, and your young men shall see visions.

Date: _____

Write the vision:

_____
_____
_____
_____
_____
_____
_____
_____
_____
_____
_____
_____
_____
_____
_____

My Vision

What stood out within the vision?

_____

_____

_____

_____

Vision Interpretation:

_____

_____

_____

_____

_____

_____

_____

_____

_____

_____

_____

_____

_____

_____

_____

_____

Fulfillment Date of Vision: _____

My Vision

Joel 2:28 (ESV)

"And it shall come to pass afterward, that I will pour out my Spirit on all flesh; your sons and your daughters shall prophesy, your old men shall dream dreams, and your young men shall see visions.

Date: _____

Write the vision:

_____
_____
_____
_____
_____
_____
_____
_____
_____
_____
_____
_____
_____
_____

My Vision

What stood out within the vision?

_____

_____

_____

_____

Vision Interpretation:

_____

_____

_____

_____

_____

_____

_____

_____

_____

_____

_____

_____

_____

_____

_____

_____

Fulfillment Date of Vision: _____

My Vision

Joel 2:28 (ESV)

"And it shall come to pass afterward, that I will pour out my Spirit on all flesh; your sons and your daughters shall prophesy, your old men shall dream dreams, and your young men shall see visions.

Date: _____

Write the vision:

_____
_____
_____
_____
_____
_____
_____
_____
_____
_____
_____
_____
_____
_____

My Vision

What stood out within the vision?

Vision Interpretation:

Fulfillment Date of Vision: _____

My Vision

Joel 2:28 (ESV)

"And it shall come to pass afterward, that I will pour out my Spirit on all flesh; your sons and your daughters shall prophesy, your old men shall dream dreams, and your young men shall see visions.

Date: _____

Write the vision:

_____
_____
_____
_____
_____
_____
_____
_____
_____
_____
_____
_____
_____
_____

My Vision

What stood out within the vision?

_____

_____

_____

_____

Vision Interpretation:

_____

_____

_____

_____

_____

_____

_____

_____

_____

_____

_____

_____

_____

_____

_____

_____

_____

Fulfillment Date of Vision: _____

Dreams – Visions – God Said

My Vision

Joel 2:28 (ESV)

"And it shall come to pass afterward, that I will pour out my Spirit on all flesh; your sons and your daughters shall prophesy, your old men shall dream dreams, and your young men shall see visions.

Date: _____

Write the vision:

_____
_____
_____
_____
_____
_____
_____
_____
_____
_____
_____
_____
_____

My Vision

What stood out within the vision?

_____

_____

_____

_____

Vision Interpretation:

_____

_____

_____

_____

_____

_____

_____

_____

_____

_____

_____

_____

_____

_____

_____

Fulfillment Date of Vision: _____

My Vision

Joel 2:28 (ESV)

"And it shall come to pass afterward, that I will pour out my Spirit on all flesh; your sons and your daughters shall prophesy, your old men shall dream dreams, and your young men shall see visions.

Date: _____

Write the vision:

_____

_____

_____

_____

_____

_____

_____

_____

_____

_____

_____

_____

_____

_____

My Vision

What stood out within the vision?

Vision Interpretation:

Fulfillment Date of Vision: _____

Dreams – Visions – God Said

My Vision

Joel 2:28 (ESV)

"And it shall come to pass afterward, that I will pour out my Spirit on all flesh; your sons and your daughters shall prophesy, your old men shall dream dreams, and your young men shall see visions.

Date: _____

Write the vision:

_____
_____
_____
_____
_____
_____
_____
_____
_____
_____
_____
_____
_____
_____
_____

My Vision

What stood out within the vision?

_____

_____

_____

_____

Vision Interpretation:

_____

_____

_____

_____

_____

_____

_____

_____

_____

_____

_____

_____

_____

_____

_____

_____

Fulfillment Date of Vision: _____

My Vision

Joel 2:28 (ESV)

"And it shall come to pass afterward, that I will pour out my Spirit on all flesh; your sons and your daughters shall prophesy, your old men shall dream dreams, and your young men shall see visions.

Date: _____

Write the vision:

_____

_____

_____

_____

_____

_____

_____

_____

_____

_____

_____

_____

_____

_____

My Vision

What stood out within the vision?

_____

_____

_____

_____

Vision Interpretation:

_____

_____

_____

_____

_____

_____

_____

_____

_____

_____

_____

_____

_____

_____

_____

_____

_____

Fulfillment Date of Vision: _____

Dreams – Visions – God Said

My Vision

Joel 2:28 (ESV)

"And it shall come to pass afterward, that I will pour out my Spirit on all flesh; your sons and your daughters shall prophesy, your old men shall dream dreams, and your young men shall see visions.

Date: _____

Write the vision:

_____
_____
_____
_____
_____
_____
_____
_____
_____
_____
_____
_____
_____
_____
_____
_____

My Vision

What stood out within the vision?

_____

_____

_____

_____

Vision Interpretation:

_____

_____

_____

_____

_____

_____

_____

_____

_____

_____

_____

_____

_____

_____

_____

_____

Fulfillment Date of Vision: _____

My Vision

Joel 2:28 (ESV)

"And it shall come to pass afterward, that I will pour out my Spirit on all flesh; your sons and your daughters shall prophesy, your old men shall dream dreams, and your young men shall see visions.

Date: _____

Write the vision:

_____
_____
_____
_____
_____
_____
_____
_____
_____
_____
_____
_____
_____
_____
_____
_____

My Vision

What stood out within the vision?

Vision Interpretation:

Fulfillment Date of Vision: _____

My Vision

Joel 2:28 (ESV)

"And it shall come to pass afterward, that I will pour out my Spirit on all flesh; your sons and your daughters shall prophesy, your old men shall dream dreams, and your young men shall see visions.

Date: _____

Write the vision:

_____
_____
_____
_____
_____
_____
_____
_____
_____
_____
_____
_____
_____
_____

My Vision

What stood out within the vision?

_____

_____

_____

_____

Vision Interpretation:

_____

_____

_____

_____

_____

_____

_____

_____

_____

_____

_____

_____

_____

_____

_____

_____

Fulfillment Date of Vision: _____

My Vision

Joel 2:28 (ESV)

"And it shall come to pass afterward, that I will pour out my Spirit on all flesh; your sons and your daughters shall prophesy, your old men shall dream dreams, and your young men shall see visions.

Date: _____

Write the vision:

_____
_____
_____
_____
_____
_____
_____
_____
_____
_____
_____
_____
_____
_____

My Vision

What stood out within the vision?

_____

_____

_____

_____

Vision Interpretation:

_____

_____

_____

_____

_____

_____

_____

_____

_____

_____

_____

_____

_____

_____

_____

_____

_____

Fulfillment Date of Vision: _____

My Vision

Joel 2:28 (ESV)

"And it shall come to pass afterward, that I will pour out my Spirit on all flesh; your sons and your daughters shall prophesy, your old men shall dream dreams, and your young men shall see visions.

Date: _____

Write the vision:

_____
_____
_____
_____
_____
_____
_____
_____
_____
_____
_____
_____
_____
_____
_____
_____

My Vision

What stood out within the vision?

_____

_____

_____

_____

Vision Interpretation:

_____

_____

_____

_____

_____

_____

_____

_____

_____

_____

_____

_____

_____

_____

_____

_____

Fulfillment Date of Vision: _____

My Vision

Joel 2:28 (ESV)

"And it shall come to pass afterward, that I will pour out my Spirit on all flesh; your sons and your daughters shall prophesy, your old men shall dream dreams, and your young men shall see visions.

Date: _____

Write the vision:

_____
_____
_____
_____
_____
_____
_____
_____
_____
_____
_____
_____
_____

My Vision

What stood out within the vision?

_____

_____

_____

_____

Vision Interpretation:

_____

_____

_____

_____

_____

_____

_____

_____

_____

_____

_____

_____

_____

_____

_____

_____

_____

Fulfillment Date of Vision: _____

My Vision

Joel 2:28 (ESV)

"And it shall come to pass afterward, that I will pour out my Spirit on all flesh; your sons and your daughters shall prophesy, your old men shall dream dreams, and your young men shall see visions.

Date: _____

Write the vision:

_____
_____
_____
_____
_____
_____
_____
_____
_____
_____
_____
_____
_____
_____

My Vision

What stood out within the vision?

Vision Interpretation:

Fulfillment Date of Vision: _____

My Vision

Joel 2:28 (ESV)

"And it shall come to pass afterward, that I will pour out my Spirit on all flesh; your sons and your daughters shall prophesy, your old men shall dream dreams, and your young men shall see visions.

Date: _____

Write the vision:

_____
_____
_____
_____
_____
_____
_____
_____
_____
_____
_____
_____
_____
_____
_____
_____

My Vision

What stood out within the vision?

Vision Interpretation:

Fulfillment Date of Vision: _____

My Vision

Joel 2:28 (ESV)

"And it shall come to pass afterward, that I will pour out my Spirit on all flesh; your sons and your daughters shall prophesy, your old men shall dream dreams, and your young men shall see visions.

Date: _____

Write the vision:

_____

_____

_____

_____

_____

_____

_____

_____

_____

_____

_____

_____

_____

_____

_____

My Vision

What stood out within the vision?

_____

_____

_____

_____

Vision Interpretation:

_____

_____

_____

_____

_____

_____

_____

_____

_____

_____

_____

_____

_____

_____

_____

_____

Fulfillment Date of Vision: _____

My Vision

Joel 2:28 (ESV)

"And it shall come to pass afterward, that I will pour out my Spirit on all flesh; your sons and your daughters shall prophesy, your old men shall dream dreams, and your young men shall see visions.

Date: _____

Write the vision:

_____
_____
_____
_____
_____
_____
_____
_____
_____
_____
_____
_____
_____
_____
_____

My Vision

What stood out within the vision?

Vision Interpretation:

Fulfillment Date of Vision: _____

My Vision

Joel 2:28 (ESV)

"And it shall come to pass afterward, that I will pour out my Spirit on all flesh; your sons and your daughters shall prophesy, your old men shall dream dreams, and your young men shall see visions.

Date: _____

Write the vision:

_____
_____
_____
_____
_____
_____
_____
_____
_____
_____
_____
_____
_____
_____
_____

My Vision

What stood out within the vision?

Vision Interpretation:

Fulfillment Date of Vision: _____

My Vision

Joel 2:28 (ESV)

"And it shall come to pass afterward, that I will pour out my Spirit on all flesh; your sons and your daughters shall prophesy, your old men shall dream dreams, and your young men shall see visions.

Date: _____

Write the vision:

_____
_____
_____
_____
_____
_____
_____
_____
_____
_____
_____
_____
_____
_____
_____

My Vision

What stood out within the vision?

_____

_____

_____

_____

Vision Interpretation:

_____

_____

_____

_____

_____

_____

_____

_____

_____

_____

_____

_____

_____

_____

_____

_____

_____

Fulfillment Date of Vision: _____

My Vision

Joel 2:28 (ESV)

"And it shall come to pass afterward, that I will pour out my Spirit on all flesh; your sons and your daughters shall prophesy, your old men shall dream dreams, and your young men shall see visions.

Date: _____

Write the vision:

_____
_____
_____
_____
_____
_____
_____
_____
_____
_____
_____
_____
_____
_____

My Vision

What stood out within the vision?

Vision Interpretation:

Fulfillment Date of Vision: _____

My Vision

Joel 2:28 (ESV)

"And it shall come to pass afterward, that I will pour out my Spirit on all flesh; your sons and your daughters shall prophesy, your old men shall dream dreams, and your young men shall see visions.

Date: _____

Write the vision:

_____
_____
_____
_____
_____
_____
_____
_____
_____
_____
_____
_____
_____
_____

My Vision

What stood out within the vision?

_____

_____

_____

_____

Vision Interpretation:

_____

_____

_____

_____

_____

_____

_____

_____

_____

_____

_____

_____

_____

_____

_____

Fulfillment Date of Vision: _____

My Vision

Joel 2:28 (ESV)

"And it shall come to pass afterward, that I will pour out my Spirit on all flesh; your sons and your daughters shall prophesy, your old men shall dream dreams, and your young men shall see visions.

Date: _____

Write the vision:

_____
_____
_____
_____
_____
_____
_____
_____
_____
_____
_____
_____
_____
_____
_____

My Vision

What stood out within the vision?

Vision Interpretation:

Fulfillment Date of Vision: _____

My Vision

Joel 2:28 (ESV)

"And it shall come to pass afterward, that I will pour out my Spirit on all flesh; your sons and your daughters shall prophesy, your old men shall dream dreams, and your young men shall see visions.

Date: _____

Write the vision:

_____
_____
_____
_____
_____
_____
_____
_____
_____
_____
_____
_____
_____
_____
_____

My Vision

What stood out within the vision?

Vision Interpretation:

Fulfillment Date of Vision: _____

My Vision

Joel 2:28 (ESV)

"And it shall come to pass afterward, that I will pour out my Spirit on all flesh; your sons and your daughters shall prophesy, your old men shall dream dreams, and your young men shall see visions.

Date: _____

Write the vision:

_____
_____
_____
_____
_____
_____
_____
_____
_____
_____
_____
_____
_____
_____

My Vision

What stood out within the vision?

_____

_____

_____

_____

Vision Interpretation:

_____

_____

_____

_____

_____

_____

_____

_____

_____

_____

_____

_____

_____

_____

_____

_____

Fulfillment Date of Vision: _____

Part Three

God Said

Jeremiah 29:11 (ESV)

For I know the plans I have for you, declares the LORD, plans for welfare and not for evil, to give you a future and a hope.

God Said

Date: _____

_____

_____

_____

_____

_____

_____

_____

God Said

Date: _____

_____

_____

_____

_____

_____

_____

_____

_____

Jeremiah 29:11 (ESV)

For I know the plans I have for you, declares the LORD, plans for welfare and not for evil, to give you a future and a hope.

God Said

Date: _____

_____

_____

_____

_____

_____

_____

_____

God Said

Date: _____

_____

_____

_____

_____

_____

_____

_____

Jeremiah 29:11 (ESV)

For I know the plans I have for you, declares the LORD, plans for welfare and not for evil, to give you a future and a hope.

God Said

Date: _____

_____
_____
_____
_____
_____
_____
_____

God Said

Date: _____

_____
_____
_____
_____
_____
_____
_____

Jeremiah 29:11 (ESV)

For I know the plans I have for you, declares the LORD, plans for welfare and not for evil, to give you a future and a hope.

God Said

Date: _____

_____
_____
_____
_____
_____
_____
_____

God Said

Date: _____

_____
_____
_____
_____
_____
_____
_____
_____

Jeremiah 29:11 (ESV)

For I know the plans I have for you, declares the LORD, plans for welfare and not for evil, to give you a future and a hope.

God Said

Date: _____

_____

_____

_____

_____

_____

_____

_____

God Said

Date: _____

_____

_____

_____

_____

_____

_____

_____

Jeremiah 29:11 (ESV)

For I know the plans I have for you, declares the LORD, plans for welfare and not for evil, to give you a future and a hope.

God Said

Date: _____

_____

_____

_____

_____

_____

_____

_____

God Said

Date: _____

_____

_____

_____

_____

_____

_____

_____

Jeremiah 29:11 (ESV)

For I know the plans I have for you, declares the LORD, plans for welfare and not for evil, to give you a future and a hope.

God Said

Date: _____

_____
_____
_____
_____
_____
_____
_____

God Said

Date: _____

_____
_____
_____
_____
_____
_____
_____
_____

Jeremiah 29:11 (ESV)

For I know the plans I have for you, declares the LORD, plans for welfare and not for evil, to give you a future and a hope.

God Said

Date: _____

_____

_____

_____

_____

_____

_____

_____

_____

God Said

Date: _____

_____

_____

_____

_____

_____

_____

_____

_____

Jeremiah 29:11 (ESV)

For I know the plans I have for you, declares the LORD, plans for welfare and not for evil, to give you a future and a hope.

God Said

Date: _____

_____
_____
_____
_____
_____
_____
_____

God Said

Date: _____

_____
_____
_____
_____
_____
_____
_____

Jeremiah 29:11 (ESV)

For I know the plans I have for you, declares the LORD, plans for welfare and not for evil, to give you a future and a hope.

God Said

Date: _____

_____
_____
_____
_____
_____
_____
_____

God Said

Date: _____

_____
_____
_____
_____
_____
_____
_____
_____

Jeremiah 29:11 (ESV)

For I know the plans I have for you, declares the LORD, plans for welfare and not for evil, to give you a future and a hope.

God Said

Date: _____

_____
_____
_____
_____
_____
_____
_____
_____

God Said

Date: _____

_____
_____
_____
_____
_____
_____
_____
_____
_____

Jeremiah 29:11 (ESV)

For I know the plans I have for you, declares the LORD, plans for welfare and not for evil, to give you a future and a hope.

God Said

Date: _____

_____
_____
_____
_____
_____
_____
_____

God Said

Date: _____

_____
_____
_____
_____
_____
_____
_____
_____

Jeremiah 29:11 (ESV)

For I know the plans I have for you, declares the LORD, plans for welfare and not for evil, to give you a future and a hope.

God Said

Date: _____

_____

_____

_____

_____

_____

_____

_____

God Said

Date: _____

_____

_____

_____

_____

_____

_____

_____

Jeremiah 29:11 (ESV)

For I know the plans I have for you, declares the LORD, plans for welfare and not for evil, to give you a future and a hope.

God Said

Date: _____

_____
_____
_____
_____
_____
_____
_____

God Said

Date: _____

_____
_____
_____
_____
_____
_____
_____

Jeremiah 29:11 (ESV)

For I know the plans I have for you, declares the LORD, plans for welfare and not for evil, to give you a future and a hope.

God Said

Date: _____

_____
_____
_____
_____
_____
_____
_____

God Said

Date: _____

_____
_____
_____
_____
_____
_____
_____
_____

Jeremiah 29:11 (ESV)

For I know the plans I have for you, declares the LORD, plans for welfare and not for evil, to give you a future and a hope.

God Said

Date: _____

_____
_____
_____
_____
_____
_____
_____
_____

God Said

Date: _____

_____
_____
_____
_____
_____
_____
_____
_____
_____

Jeremiah 29:11 (ESV)

For I know the plans I have for you, declares the LORD, plans for welfare and not for evil, to give you a future and a hope.

God Said

Date: _____

_____
_____
_____
_____
_____
_____
_____

God Said

Date: _____

_____
_____
_____
_____
_____
_____
_____

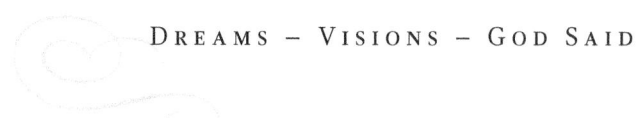

Jeremiah 29:11 (ESV)

For I know the plans I have for you, declares the LORD, plans for welfare and not for evil, to give you a future and a hope.

God Said

Date: _____

_____
_____
_____
_____
_____
_____
_____

God Said

Date: _____

_____
_____
_____
_____
_____
_____
_____

Jeremiah 29:11 (ESV)

For I know the plans I have for you, declares the LORD, plans for welfare and not for evil, to give you a future and a hope.

God Said

Date: _____

_____
_____
_____
_____
_____
_____
_____

God Said

Date: _____

_____
_____
_____
_____
_____
_____
_____
_____

Jeremiah 29:11 (ESV)

For I know the plans I have for you, declares the LORD, plans for welfare and not for evil, to give you a future and a hope.

God Said

Date: _____

_____
_____
_____
_____
_____
_____
_____

God Said

Date: _____

_____
_____
_____
_____
_____
_____
_____
_____

Jeremiah 29:11 (ESV)

For I know the plans I have for you, declares the LORD, plans for welfare and not for evil, to give you a future and a hope.

God Said

Date: _____

_____

_____

_____

_____

_____

_____

_____

God Said

Date: _____

_____

_____

_____

_____

_____

_____

_____

_____

Jeremiah 29:11 (ESV)

For I know the plans I have for you, declares the LORD, plans for welfare and not for evil, to give you a future and a hope.

God Said

Date: _____

_____
_____
_____
_____
_____
_____
_____

God Said

Date: _____

_____
_____
_____
_____
_____
_____
_____

Jeremiah 29:11 (ESV)

For I know the plans I have for you, declares the LORD, plans for welfare and not for evil, to give you a future and a hope.

God Said

Date: _____

_____
_____
_____
_____
_____
_____
_____

God Said

Date: _____

_____
_____
_____
_____
_____
_____
_____
_____

Jeremiah 29:11 (ESV)

For I know the plans I have for you, declares the LORD, plans for welfare and not for evil, to give you a future and a hope.

God Said

Date: _____

_____
_____
_____
_____
_____
_____
_____
_____

God Said

Date: _____

_____
_____
_____
_____
_____
_____
_____
_____

Jeremiah 29:11 (ESV)

For I know the plans I have for you, declares the LORD, plans for welfare and not for evil, to give you a future and a hope.

God Said

Date: _____

_____
_____
_____
_____
_____
_____
_____

God Said

Date: _____

_____
_____
_____
_____
_____
_____
_____

Jeremiah 29:11 (ESV)

For I know the plans I have for you, declares the LORD, plans for welfare and not for evil, to give you a future and a hope.

God Said

Date: _____

_____
_____
_____
_____
_____
_____
_____

God Said

Date: _____

_____
_____
_____
_____
_____
_____
_____
_____

Jeremiah 29:11 (ESV)

For I know the plans I have for you, declares the LORD, plans for welfare and not for evil, to give you a future and a hope.

God Said

Date: _____

_____
_____
_____
_____
_____
_____
_____
_____

God Said

Date: _____

_____
_____
_____
_____
_____
_____
_____
_____

Jeremiah 29:11 (ESV)

For I know the plans I have for you, declares the LORD, plans for welfare and not for evil, to give you a future and a hope.

God Said

Date: _____

_____

_____

_____

_____

_____

_____

_____

God Said

Date: _____

_____

_____

_____

_____

_____

_____

_____

_____

Jeremiah 29:11 (ESV)

For I know the plans I have for you, declares the LORD, plans for welfare and not for evil, to give you a future and a hope.

God Said

Date: _____

_____
_____
_____
_____
_____
_____
_____
_____

God Said

Date: _____

_____
_____
_____
_____
_____
_____
_____
_____

Jeremiah 29:11 (ESV)

For I know the plans I have for you, declares the LORD, plans for welfare and not for evil, to give you a future and a hope.

God Said

Date: _____

_____

_____

_____

_____

_____

_____

_____

God Said

Date: _____

_____

_____

_____

_____

_____

_____

_____

_____

Jeremiah 29:11 (ESV)

For I know the plans I have for you, declares the LORD, plans for welfare and not for evil, to give you a future and a hope.

God Said

Date: _____

_____
_____
_____
_____
_____
_____
_____

God Said

Date: _____

_____
_____
_____
_____
_____
_____
_____
_____

About The Author

Servant Stacy (Apostle) is a born native of Trinidad & Tobago but resides in Philadelphia, USA, for over 20 years. She is a mother of two young men and a grandmother of 1. Servant Stacy (Apostle) is the founder of Servant Stacy International Deliverance Ministries. She has been saved for over 27 years. She believes that we should obey God's commands at all costs. She lives by 1 Peter 1:16 to the best of her ability.

www.ingramcontent.com/pod-product-compliance
Lightning Source LLC
Chambersburg PA
CBHW081738100526
44592CB00015B/2223